DEANN KRUEMPEL

Candles and Mirrors

First edition

ISBN: 978-1-952891-16-8

This book was professionally typeset on Reedsy.
Find out more at reedsy.com

Contents

I

Dedication

Candles and Mirrors is dedicated to small-town newspapers. These pillars of communities strive to connect people and events. They report local news and print photos, which are often clipped and saved by proud loved ones. Local newspapers have recorded history that may not be printed in any other document. Editors and reporters work tirelessly and often with little compensation or recognition.
Thank you!

1

Life, Light and Reflections

The huge scoreboard ticked away the final minutes of the last quarter. Two small schools, dead set on winning their district tournament, had run neck and neck the entire game. Buzzers and whistles blared loudly in the Huron arena that night.

The net swished like a breeze as an Erwin player put in a stellar shot from beyond the free throw line. The score was tied.

Feet pounded on the bleachers. Every fan stood. Some clasped their hands as they watched sons, brothers, friends. Screams from the crowd drowned the chants of the cheerleaders. Seconds ticked away on the clock.

The Erwin guards bolted down the court to block their opponents. Arms lifted high. A player pressed forward, reaching frantically to steal the ball, but the other player held on. The referee's whistle shrilled above the noise of the fans, calling for a jump-ball.

The officials lined the players around the free-throw line to set up a jump to decide who got the ball. Though three inches shorter, the Erwin player got the tip and the ball landed in the hands of our brother, who deftly laid it through the hoop above. Fans gasped. Others groaned. Donald had scored two points for the other team!

The Erwin coach stepped out on the floor and signaled time-out. I can only imagine the crushing disappointment my brother must have felt at that moment, blaming himself for letting down his teammates, his friends.

Uniforms drenched in sweat, the five walked to the huddle. The few players left on the bleachers sidled in to show their support.

I don't know what the coach said to those young men nearly 60 years ago, but the story of a fellow player's faith and what went on to happen at that basketball game lives on in the hearts of all of my siblings. His nickname was Willie. Unwavering, his eyes met Don's. "Don't worry about it. You will score for us and we will win this game!"

As it turned out, he did and they did.

Pulitzer Prize winner Edith Wharton once said, "There are two ways of spreading light: to be the candle or the mirror that reflects it."

The above story stands out in my mind as a perfect example of light and reflection—a great beginning for a new year of stories. All of my siblings remember either the game or the re-telling. Even after all these years, their voices falter, their eyes flood.

Consider all the light that shines from the story. A friend's encouragement that may have made the difference. Our brother's determination to win for the team as well as redeem himself. The happy ending made even better because it outshined the shadow, the mistake. Can we all empathize?

I cannot find any more details about that game. Something was said about the refs lining up the players incorrectly. (Though I was only three at the time and remember nothing, all these years later I really want to blame the refs!) But our father would have taught all six of us, even after the 95th telling of the story that we are ultimately accountable for our mistakes.

Can such a memory cast a ray of light in our present world? Every one of us has stories to tell. Even the saddest memories can be a light to someone who needs encouragement to power through rough times. It is my prayer that in some small way the stories will inspire you.

Be the candle. Be the mirror.

Donald's picture from the Erwin yearbook.

The Erwin basketball team. Donald is top row, third player from left. Lowell Gilbertson, shown holding the basketball, later married our sister, Deloris.

2

Ties That Bind

It was just big enough—my very own secret hiding place! Two or three bales had been pulled from the straw pile in front of the barn, leaving a small cave, a perfect hangout. It was dry and warm inside; the barn blocked the South Dakota wind. Momma Kitty jumped up behind me and for a half hour she purred in perfect understanding as I poured out the typical catastrophic woes of a nine-year-old girl, stories inspired by the clean, earthy smell of oat straw. I knew our private spot would not last long. Tomorrow fresh bedding would be needed and the guys would grab more bales from the pile.

A barn door clicked shut and Dad walked by, just below. I pulled my boots inside, not wanting to give away the secret. As I snuggled in, my mitten caught on the tan colored twine that bound the bale together, reminding me of last summer when this stack came about.

"Delmer, you and DeAnn take the hay rack out to the oat field and pick up the bales. There are only about 90 left." Dad's confidence in my tractor-driving ability far exceeded my own. I was shaking in my tennis shoes.

I sat quietly next to my brother on the tractor seat as we headed down the road to the oat field, the bale loader and rack rattling behind us on the gravel. "You'll be alright, DeAnn. You just have to line up the bales between those guides on the loader. If you hit it right, the bale will ride right up to me." Easy for him to say!

Dad and Donald had taken off the chopper from the back end of the pull-behind combine. The oat straw was easy to pick up and bind into square bales. Back then the straw was as important as the oats. Plenty of dry, warm bedding kept cattle, hogs and chickens happy and healthy during winter months when they were confined to barns and coops.

The bales formed parallel (mostly) lines through the field. Delmer got me started and I nudged the clutch forward on the John Deere 520. I puffed a sigh of relief as the first few bales fit into the guides and traveled up the elevator chains. They slid to a stop on the platform just above the hay rack. Delmer grabbed them by the twine ties and carried them back to begin the pile on the hay rack.

Of course, life can never be easy. The next bale was somewhat askew, certainly not in a perfect line to follow into the loader. Visions of broken bales danced in my head. I didn't look back because I figured Delmer would expect me to steer the tractor into place and expertly reel in that bale. I yanked back on the clutch to stop the tractor and scurried down to re-position the straw block. Only when I was certain it would easily head into the chute did I climb back up to the tractor seat.

The day wore on. I stopped to move a lot of bales. I envisioned my brother chewing on a straw of oats waiting for the next golden chunk to hurtle up to him. Maybe he sat on a bale as he waited. Maybe he took a nap.

We got the bales picked up and headed home. Delmer didn't complain about how long it took or how many times we stopped.

When we pulled into the yard, he maneuvered the rack next to the barn to unload.

I am pretty sure Dad checked his watch, but he never asked what took us so long to bring home the straw bales that day.

Even more amazing was the fact that Mamma Kitty and I kept our secret hiding place for a long time that winter. For some strange reason, when the guys needed a bale, they pulled it from the other side of the stack.

3

Stirring Up Memories

They arrived in buggies, wagons and on horseback, ready to work. Some stoked the fire with hemlock and pine. Some lugged crocks of cider to the huge cauldron. Many sat on stumps or logs and began to peel and core. Baskets of fruit were dumped into the boiling liquid. The farmer brought out his handmade stirrer, a wooden paddle attached at a right angle to a smooth ten-foot pole. It was like a hoe with a long blade. He had bored large holes into the board so the liquid could pass through, avoiding sloshing spills. The person in charge of stirring stood far back from the hot, smoky fire and swirled the paddle through the steaming kettle. The workers took turns stirring for fifteen minutes, constantly scraping the bottom and sides. Not once could they stop. Stopping meant scorching and scorching meant they would have to dump the kettle and start over.

The farmer's family had worked for days, picking baskets of apples from their orchard and hauling them to the yard next to the fire pit. The wife had scrubbed the giant kettle and her husband helped hang it from the sturdy frame he had built. They had extended the invitation at Sunday services: Apple Butter Bee on Friday!

Apple butter originated in Germany and the Netherlands; when the immigrants sailed to America they brought the recipe with them. The above scene was typical in New England in the late 1800s. The neighborhood bee was a social event, but also a crucial means of preserving the harvest to survive the harsh winters.

The Pennsylvania Dutch boiled down apple cider, then added peeled and quartered apples to be cooked to a very thick consistency. Some added spices, but one old recipe I discovered claimed no spices where needed; the apples and cider formed a delicious thick mass that "kept in crocks for years."

Seventy years later…Mom's daughters gathered around her in our farm kitchen. She added a few chunks of wood and a handful of cobs to the woodstove. The night before, the family had brought in a basket of apples from the orchard—windfalls, crab apples, small fruit from the tree. We washed and plopped them into the big canning kettle. Mom carried the canner to the stove and added water. Soon it began to boil. Once the apples were cooked, she hefted the kettle to the table and we began running them through the food mill. One sister ladled, one cranked. When the good parts of the apple had squished through the mill into the bowl below, we dumped the nearly-dry mass of peel, seeds and cores into the pail for the chickens and ladled in more apples.

When all the pulp was pressed out, Mom dumped it into the big kettle and added water, sugar, cinnamon and salt. This went on the back burner and slowly began to simmer. Mom got out her long wooden spoon and stirred the liquid. Deloris, Darlene and Dorothy took turns stirring occasionally. As the mixture thickened and steamed, a heavenly aroma filled the house, reminding us to stir more often. When the mixture thickened to the Goldilocks consistency, just right, we ladled some into jars that would be stashed for winter. Our mouths watered as we gazed at the savory goodness that remained in the kettle.

Mom's recipe says "simmer ¾ hour." My siblings and I agree that it was much longer than that. Maybe it was. Or maybe it just seemed like forever because we couldn't wait to spread that amazing apple butter on fresh, homemade bread and enjoy the feast!

Mom's Recipe for Apple Butter
4 quarts apples
3 cups sugar

4 cups water

2 Tablespoons ground cinnamon

2 teaspoons salt

Wash and quarter the apples, do not peel them or remove the core. Put into a preserving kettle with water. Bring to a boil rapidly. Simmer until tender. Mash through a strainer and return to fire. Add sugar, cinnamon and salt and simmer ¾ hour. Pack in jars and seal. I usually put wax on before I seal the jars.

4

The Tiny Wooden Bridge

We all have them. Pictures from the past that are so clear in our minds it is as if we saw them only yesterday. At any given time, with the smallest reminder, an image can flash before us.

Our mother stood barely five feet tall, including the wedge heels on her size-five leather shoes. But in my mind's eye she always fit perfectly in her kitchen. Whether she stood at the sink, the stove or the table, a sense of rightness emanated from her as she worked. Invariably, I remember a smile on her face. And more often than not, she held a wooden spoon in her left hand.

The spoon had a long handle, and by the time I came along it was well-seasoned; the bowl and lower part were stained darker than the top. Mom reached for her favorite spoon when she brought out the big earthenware bowl to mix cookies. The wooden tool blended many cups of flour into yeasty batter that was turned into bread, rolls or tuffies. She chose the spoon from the drawer when she mixed meat loaf. Her bare left arm moved over the steaming cast-iron fry pan, using the spoon to turn chunks of browning hamburger. Later the utensil swirled through the kettle of chili, making sure it did not scorch to the bottom. The long handle peeked from the top of the canning kettle, ready to stir the thick apple butter that softly bubbled around it.

I wish I would have asked our mother where she got that beloved spoon.

Did her mother present it to her just-married daughter with a few bowls and pans? "These will get you started in your own kitchen, Mabel." Or, "I have extra things I will share."

Or did Mom and Dad use some of their meager savings to purchase things she knew they would need to set up housekeeping? What would a wooden spoon have cost in 1939?

That spoon spanned a lot of years and stirred up a bounty of wonderful memories. Much smaller hands often reached for the same spoon, learning hands. Deloris, Darlene, Dorothy and I stood at our mother's side as she happily taught us what every girl should know, often handing over the tasks of mixing, blending and scraping. Since Mom was left-handed, one edge wore down slightly more than the other. Darlene and Dorothy contributed to the left-handed flattening.

Back then I never noticed the wear, nor did I consider how very precious that spoon was. But I will never forget how right it seemed when Mom held it; she was happiest when she was in her kitchen mixing up good things to feed her family.

The spoon bridged generations and today belongs to my sister, Dorothy. Nearly eighty years later that same wooden spoon is still mixing, stirring and blending. From apple cake to brownies to chili, another loving hand continues to wear down the left side. And I am very certain as she blends and mixes memories for her family, my sister is smiling.

Two of Mom's wooden spoons, still stirring up memories at Dorothy's house.
Thank you, Dorothy!

5

Living By the Rules

"Children should be seen, not heard." Both of our parents were raised by the strict rule; when adults were present, youngsters were not allowed to speak unless spoken to. Our parents carried on the tradition to a certain extent with their own children.

My siblings remember the family law: when we were among adults, whether in our home or visiting elsewhere, we were expected to listen quietly. As the youngest, most spoiled child, I don't remember such imposed silence. I did understand that I was to show respect to all adults and that I should never interrupt when someone else was speaking.

Growing up on the farm in South Dakota, we had other rules. Work before play. No shooting baskets or tire swing adventures when chores waited. If Mom was outside carrying feed to the chickens or inside preparing supper, we had better be helping in some way. If Dad was picking corn in the field, the rest of the family pitched in wherever needed. Blackie knew she would be milked twice a day at the same time. The livestock never went hungry. Neither did we.

Everyone sat at the supper table. After saying grace together, Dad helped himself to the bowls of food and passed them around. We were expected to consider the rest of the family; to empty the gravy bowl when five more were waiting would have been frowned upon. Eating the vegetable was mandatory, even if just a spoonful. No dessert allowed unless we cleaned up our plates.

And we all loved dessert!

Delmer recalls one of Dad's suppertime rules: No jam on our first slice of bread. We could slather plum jam or apple butter on the second slice to our heart's content, but only butter was allowed on the first. I am still trying to figure out the reasoning behind that one!

The supper table conversation may have touched on Dorothy's purple ribbon no-bake chocolate cookies, Delmer's home run at the Legion baseball tournament, why I felt the need to run away from Bible School or the thistles that needed hoeing in the south pasture. It was also a time when the folks reminisced of their own growing-up years. We stayed at the table until everyone was finished. Before we could slide off our chair, each addressed our father, "Please, may I be excused?"

Rules followed us wherever we went, including school. From day one, each of us understood that if we got into trouble at school, we would be in far deeper trouble at home. The rule was pretty effective except for those times when the folks never found out, but that's another story!

The first thing we did when we came home from school was change into everyday clothes. It was important to take care of what we had. After supper, homework reigned supreme over TV, games or books, at least in our parents' eyes. However, if I sat in the right spot at the kitchen table, I could lean back and see the TV in the living room.

"Turn off the light when you leave the room." "Hold the door for others to enter first." "Offer to carry heavy packages." "Always say please and thank you."

Most of our rules were not unique to our family, and though we may have grumbled (very quietly), we understood the reasoning behind them. Respect others. Life is easier when everyone pitches in. Nothing should be wasted.

A lifetime later as I reflect on those growing-up-time rules, I realize they had a part in making us what we are today. We learned teamwork, responsibility, persistence, accountability and the value of hard work. As for that one about children being seen and not heard—well, I am really glad to be the youngest!

6

Those Who Have Ears, Let Them Smile!

The sun flickered between the rows as we drove slowly by. Tall, tan stalks stood in perfect formation. Each spire sported a pointy sunburst, the dry flower of the tassel. Long tapered cylinders clothed in tawny jackets hung heavily from the thick stems.

All at once Dad pulled the car to the side of the road. He was out the door, down the ditch and between the barbed wires quicker than we could say "corn meal mush!" Through her open window, Mom and I watched the stalks bend as he moved farther into the field. Amid the rustle of crisp dry leaves, we heard snapping and ripping sounds. Minutes later Dad emerged, carrying three long, golden ears, husks flaring from their bases. Mom shook her head a bit, but her eyes sparkled as her smiling farmer proudly laid them on her lap.

For around 20 years, those whole ears of corn played a huge role on our South Dakota farm. When the folks were married in 1939, they harvested their corn crop by hand, walking between the rows, tearing off each ear and throwing it into the horse-drawn wooden wagon with attached side boards. They could fill two wagons in a day. When they brought in the second load, Dad emptied the wagon while Mom milked the cows. Their corn harvest fed the livestock and cook stove until next year's crop came in.

Years later, our father told the story of how Mom was known to be one of the fastest pickers around. She could rip the ear off the stalk, tear off the husk and throw it in the wagon in record time. Their leather wrist straps with attached husking pegs hung from beams in our basement for years.

Time passed and the corn fields grew larger along with our herds and flocks. Technology grew with them. A tractor now pulled a two-row John Deere corn picker. The loaden ears it picked and husked dropped directly into the new flare-box metal wagon behind. Mom and the boys unloaded the crop into the elevator that carried the ears up into slatted cribs to dry. Years when spring arrived late, some of the corn was late maturing. Delmer recalls our mother standing at the bottom hopper and watching for wet ears. She grabbed the undented corn and threw it into a pile. Delmer used his trusty little red wagon to haul it to the barn to be savored by the milk cow.

It was the kids' job to shell corn for the chickens every night. The metal hand-crank sheller sat next to the crib. We loaded the hopper on top of the sheller with a pile of ears and dropped them, one by one, into the chute. If two of us worked together, the job went a lot faster. I remember feeding in the ears while Delmer cranked away. Golden kernels fell into the bucket underneath. Rough red cobs popped out the back. Later these cobs provided fuel for Mom's cook stove. Nothing was wasted.

Today, eight to eighteen-row combines hurtle through ripe corn fields, quickly removing ears and husks and stripping kernels from the cobs. Stalks, leaves and cobs are chopped and returned to the soil. Wagons and semi-trucks haul thousands of bushels of the loose, clean kernels to bins or elevators. Fields are finished in a matter of hours.

In less than 100 years, the methods of harvesting as well as the uses for corn crops have changed drastically. But I am pretty sure farmers still search their fields for the longest, fattest ears they can find. And I know they still smile.

The hand-crank corn sheller now resides at Delmer's.

7

A Thing of Beauty is a Joy Forever

I knelt on the carpet next to her easy chair. She held the round frame in her hands and guided me as I pushed the needle through the white fabric. "You can do it. You just need to keep trying." Mom had demonstrated the basic embroidery stitches on the flour sack dish towel. She had ironed on a simple design, a rose with leaves. Her metal hoop circled the image and held it tight. My learning stitches were crooked and uneven, but the red flower began to stand out, a pretty decoration on the bottom of the towel.

She called it her "fancy work." Embroidery and crochet. There was always a project waiting for our mother when she sat in her chair at the end of the day.

The dime store carried plenty of plain cotton towels and iron-on patterns. Mom embroidered days-of-the-week dish towels with puppies, birds or fruit. It didn't take long for a set of seven to be ready for an upcoming shower gift.

Lee Wards and Herrschners catalogs were like Wish Books for Mom. She would page through and mark her favorites. Ultimately, the finished projects became gifts for family and friends.

Embroidered pillow cases made a special wedding gift, especially if a lovely crocheted edging fanned out next to the floral bouquet or sleeping kittens that sparkled on the starched, ironed cases. Fabric scraps sewn into squares made handy potholders, but they needed something pretty stitched on.

Mother's sisters also loved their crafts. Every year Aunt Julia tucked a pretty hanky in my birthday card. One was a sheer white linen on which she had embroidered tiny white flowers. A half-inch edge of crocheted turquoise lace surrounded the delicate square.

Aprons were everyday necessities. Of course, women sewed their own, but they also made them to give away. Mom would scan through issues of *Work Basket* magazine for cross-stitch patterns to add a charming trim to the hems and pockets of gingham aprons.

Most of these homemade items were basic garments or household necessities. Almost all were doomed for stains, sweat, grime, cooking burns and fading from many washings. But for some reason, it was important to those women to make things pretty. Why? Was it because they had lived through the Great Depression and World War II? The rationing, the sadness, the worry? That somehow creating something beautiful made a lasting, tangible symbol of love and joy?

For decades, Mom continued to embroider, crochet and give. Then one day, more than 40 years after she had patiently taught me those first embroidery stitches, my daughter and I stood next to her hospital bed. Her speech was impaired and her right hand no longer worked.

"I wonder if I can still do my fancy work." She tried to turn her head to the white bundle of fabric on the bedside table. I reached for the flour sack dish towel, bound in the familiar round hoop. A little hen, surrounded by baby chicks waited to be filled with color. I held the hoop so she could reach the threaded needle. I prayed. With one shaking hand she took a stitch.

"You can do it, Mom. You just have to keep trying."

She did. She recovered from the stroke and her loving hands went on to create more beautiful things. I wonder if she knew how much joy they would bring her family. I wonder if she knew we will treasure them forever.

Mom stitching on one of her quilts

8

White Riders in the Sky

"Make sure you get them all out of the trees." The final glow of the South Dakota sunset peeked under the windmill as I headed to what we called the brooder house—the home of 50 Plymouth Rock and leghorn pullets since their chickhood. Mom loved her chickens and did not want to lose any to raccoons or other nighttime predators.

For some reason a few of the white leghorns felt the need to spend their nights under the stars. It was often my job to gently persuade them out of the trees and into the coop. I scanned the nearly-bare branches and counted seven feathered freedom fighters hunkered down on various branches throughout the gnarled boxelder.

Hope springs eternal, especially in the heart of a nine-year-old. Maybe those girls would cooperate tonight and fly out with a little branch shaking. Two glided to the ground, then scurried to the small coop door. The others lifted their wings slightly, but remained in place, as if riding a ship at sea.

Plan B: the six-foot branch we kept next to the pasture fence, just beyond the trees. I grabbed that stick and quietly sneaked under the branches. I would take them by surprise! A few slight prods ended in rather noisy flights, wild cackling and three more white feather balls rolling home.

The last lingering loafers flashed evil, beady eyes, daring me to disturb their plan for a treetop slumber party. I yelled at them. "Stupid chickens! Do you want to die?" The two prattled quietly, likely figuring I would give up.

All remnants of daylight were quickly fading, along with my chances of getting those girls safely inside. The situation called for desperate measures. A short section of two-by-four waited next to the tree trunk. I figured it was there for a reason. I grabbed that chunk of wood and hurled it up at those ornery critters! They seemed to chuckle as the missile soared over their heads. The next throw I connected with one. "Ha! So there!" She seemed confused at first as she hit the ground, but eventually dashed for the door.

One tenacious teen remained on a limb fifteen feet above. Darkness quickly took over, as did my imagination of scary things in the night. My heart pounded as I retrieved the piece of wood. I sucked in a deep breath and I threw that wooden weapon with all my might, right up at that chicken. Miracles happen! Suddenly, a squawking, wing-flailing bundle hurtled down wildly, crash-landing only a few yards away.

I stared at that downed chicken as she laid there, her feet sprawled out behind her. My tummy started to hurt; I envisioned carrying the broken creature to Mom and repenting for my impatience. I slowly stepped forward and bent to pick her up. That faking fowl jumped up and raced inside!

I heaved a sigh of relief that all the pullets were finally safe. I was also very thankful that this chore was done. Tomorrow night the family would carry the young pullets up to the henhouse, where fresh clean straw awaited them. My tree-shaking, chicken-crashing days were over for the year. Life was good.

But as I strode back to the house, a horrible thought struck me, like a rotten egg to the solar plexus. Soon those young pullets would morph into cranky old clucks—clucks who squawked and pecked small hands searching for eggs.

Visions of a short piece of two-by-four danced in my head!

9

Ankle Deep in History

Margaret blushed crimson as she realized that her dress had lifted above her ankles for a moment. What would her mother think of such impropriety? Though the scene is from a historical fiction novel, it accurately portrayed the social norm of the late 1800s. Women were to keep their ankles covered.

Step forward 50 plus years. Many events had gone down in history while hemlines went up. After two wars and the Great Depression, years of doing without material comforts, Americans were ready for cheerful fashion and fun. What could impact fun levels more than what people wore on their feet? Thick-cuffed white socks flashed brightly on top of black and white saddle shoes on teens who swooned while Sinatra crooned. Bobby socks! Named after the "bobbed" hairstyle that was the trend at the time, these short, cuffed socks began as a symbol of teenage rebellion. *Newsweek* magazine initially defined "bobby soxers" as female juvenile delinquents. The prevailing stereotype, however, depicted them as phone-gabbing, music-loving teens in swirling skirts. Bobby socks first gained popularity in the 1940s and reached their peak in the 1950s.

My sisters wore bobby socks and saddle shoes. Add poodle skirts to the fashion statement of the era. By the time my sock-wearing, style-caring days came along, the flared felt skirts, black and white shoes and poofy-ankle socks were outdated. (I miss all the fun!) Instead, cable-knit knee-socks which inevitably sagged to my ankles two minutes into recess, quietly whispered my fashion statement and I considered Mr. Sinatra an old guy with greasy, short hair!

Eventually, women wore pants. Trouser socks kept ankles covered and came in basic neutral colors to coordinate with the pants. Brown socks with brown pants. Black socks with black or gray pants. To overstep the fashion bounds of color drew unwanted attention to the ankles.

Then trends totally turned around and suddenly socks sought to be seen! Argyle prints, wild Waldo stripes, groovy flowers and cutesy cats covered ankles across the country. Then cropped up something even more scandalous—mismatched socks! It didn't matter if one sock was Christmas plaid and the other summery-yellow. Anything goes! Parents rejoiced. They no longer had to spend hours hunting for socks the dryer ate. They no longer needed to match colors or styles. The new norm was "open drawer, pick two."

At my age I find it difficult to step into the far-fetched fad. Mostly, I prefer that my socks match. Since it was time to wrap up my winter wardrobe and prepare for the cold months ahead, I recently visited the hosiery section of my favorite department store. I wanted soft, warm, fuzzy, knee-high socks. Comfort socks. Chicken soup for the soles kind of socks.

There were rows upon rows of socks in every color and length. Cotton, wool, spandex blend. Obviously, consumers take ankle fashion seriously. Suddenly, I spotted a whole row of "no-show" socks! Seriously? Is it sinful for one's socks to show? Does anyone but me care about cold ankles?

In the next 50 years, will foot fashion hit the floor or tread lightly? Will ankles again be covered in modesty? What will they think of next? Could be it would knock our socks off!

10

Not By a Long Stretch

Today's trendy teens are missing all the fun.

Imagine this: women lined up outside stores, waiting to snag just one. But supplies were short. Coveting crowds grew angry. Riots ensued. Though the scene may seem a stretch of the imagination, it really happened. There was a time when American women went to great lengths to get—a pair of nylon stockings.

Nylon, the first synthetic fiber made totally from chemicals, was created in 1930 by DuPont, who claimed its new fiber was fine as a spider's web and strong as steel. Nylon stockings were introduced at the New York World's Fair in 1939. Women loved them! I can envision our mother and her sisters in a nightgown huddle, plotting a way to save up enough to buy a pair. At more than a dollar, that would have been no easy task. (At the time a loaf of bread cost ten cents.)

Their fashion fling was short-lived because in 1942 nylon went to war. Instead of knitting nylons, factories produced tents, parachutes and ropes for our soldiers. After the war, the factories began to make nylon stockings again. Women rejoiced!

I recall Mom and my sisters wearing the shimmering leg coverings. By the time I graduated from knee socks, panty hose had been invented. I missed all the fun!

Yes, fashion changes have taken great leaps and I cannot help but lament all the mind-bending experiences today's adolescents are missing. Never in history have women been so innovative and sacrificial as during the Age of Nylons.

From the get-go they overcame overwhelming obstacles. The first hose were thigh-high flat-cut pieces of fabric sewn together down the back of the leg. That sewing-together made a seam, a dark stripe that ran down the back and joined a triangle under the foot where the end was stitched shut. "Is my seam straight?" women questioned as they tried to twist and bend. New yoga poses were created.

Stockings had no elastic. Something had to hold them up. Alas, the comfort and convenience of the illustrious garter belt! A thin strip of fabric encircled the waist. From each side hung two lengths of elastic. A metal clasp fastened over a round button and hung from the elastic strands. Women attached nylons into the clasp garters. Garter-gaping was disgraceful. Crossing of legs was invented, thus eliminating guarding of one garter.

Some situations required drastic measures. Garter belt missing? Bare legs were not an option. Rubber bands to the rescue! Circulation was cut off. Limb loss loomed, but fashion reigned.

Holding nylons up was only part of the drama. Nylon fibers were knit together in such a way that a tiny hole or a snag caused a "run," an obvious stripe of holey horror that quickly snaked its way up or down the leg. Helpful friends snidely sniped, "You've got a run in your nylons."

Not to be deterred, girls fashioned run-resisting recipes. Hairspray, glue and nail polish to the rescue! A dab applied at the snag site sometimes saved the day. The circle of skin that peeled away that night was a small sacrifice.

Later, panty hose captivated young women with new adventures: A waist-band that reached to the armpits. A low-hanging crotch that took foot dragging to a whole new level. Saggy, baggy ankles.

But times have changed. Today bare legs are the fashion. Women no longer shimmy into those beloved gossamer stockings. Too bad. They are missing all the fun!

11

Horses Can't Play Basketball!

"Come on, DeAnn. It'll be fun!" My brother strode happily to the barn, the basketball bouncing on the frozen ground before him as he adeptly switched from right hand to left. I followed reluctantly; the feeling of dread chilled me more than the December temperatures. I couldn't hit the broad side of a barn. That was saying something considering the hoop was attached to the broad side of the barn.

Delmer stopped at the imaginary free-throw line. He bounced the ball three times, aimed at the hoop and shot. Swish! The net fluttered for a second, but the rim remained as still as stone. He grabbed the ball and went in for a lay-up. Another good one. His braces sparkled as he turned to me. Show-off!

I groaned and hightailed to the house. It was one thing to shoot hoops with my brother, but on his Wilt Chamberlain days, it teetered on self-torture. "Aww, come on, DeAnn. Let's play a game of HORSE."

As if that would entice me. Then he added, "I will start with two letters." I stopped and considered.

"Four and I will play. And I get to shoot first." I may not have been much of a basketball player, but I wasn't stupid. We compromised at three.

I stood just to the right of the hoop, about as close as I could get. I tried to aim just above the hoop, hoping it would ricochet in. I am such a dreamer.

Delmer took control. He put in a shot a few feet back and to the left. I shuffled to the same spot and attempted a similar shot. I missed. That gave me an H. And it gave my brother the ball. He dribbled three times on the packed dirt and put in a right-handed layup. I gave him the dirtiest look I could muster, bounced three times as I strode to the spot under the hoop. I aimed and tossed. Miracles happen! It went in.

That meant I got the next shot. I dribbled from the straw bale stack to the corner of the barn and then to the free-throw line. "Sometime today, maybe?" My patient brother rolled his eyes and a foul idea hurtled into my brain.

Grinning wickedly, I took two steps forward, I narrowed my eyes and stared at that hoop. I sucked in a big breath, and with both hands grasping the ball, I bent over, lowering it to the ground between my shoes and lobbed it up. Unbelievably, I made another one.

Rules of the game require the second player to attempt the same shot from the same spot. Poor Delmer cleared his throat. Ah, the humiliation, the agony! But he dipped the ball down and tossed it up—right into the hoop.

The game went down-hill from there. My brother didn't miss. I begged for mercy. After all, I was a lot farther from the hoop than he was. The game soon ended. In spite of my three-letter advantage, I missed five shots he had made and ultimately spelled HORSE.

Our older brother Donald taught Delmer the game, but I am not sure how it originated. NBA players were known to play it. Why was it named HORSE? Because horses can't play basketball!

After that trouncing I did some practicing when my brother was not around. I tried shooting from far away and five feet in front of the hoop. I tried the backward over-the-head shot. The Globetrotters would have been proud!

A month later, my brother trudged by the barn in the snow. I waited, basketball under my arm. "Hey Delmer, want to play a game of HORSE? Come on. It will be fun."

We played H.O.R.S.E. in front of the barn. The basketball hoop was attached near the center.

12

Nothing But the Best

It resembled a chubby bear, one that you could imagine if you stared up at a poofy cloud. Though far from round, Mom said it would work. She placed her smallest pie tin just next to the huge floury board we used for rolling. I plunked down the heavy rolling pin I had swiped back and forth over the clump of dough, creating a thin, even layer. (OK, maybe not very thin. And quite bumpy; imagine the bear's tummy.)

"Now you just need to get it into the pan," Mom smiled patiently. I reached for the top part of the potential crust as I had seen our mother do many times. My fingers lifted one ear and the top of the head to fold and place in the pie pan. It sort-of peeled away from the board until I got to the tummy part. There it stuck. I groaned as a gaping hole stared at me and it broke apart. "That happens to me sometimes, too. You just roll it out again."

My three older sisters and I all learned the art of pie making at our mother's side. Pie was the standard dessert at our house for Sunday dinners, Thanksgiving, Christmas and any time invited guests sat around our big kitchen table. The lovely spice-scent of apple pie in the oven often greeted us on a cold winter day, but Mom taught us how to make pumpkin, lemon meringue, coconut cream, banana cream, sour cream raisin, mincemeat and more.

While she rolled, patted and crimped, she reminisced of her growing-up days. "When we had threshers, we made seven or eight pies." I envisioned

Mom and my dear aunts, Lilly, Julia, Ida and Emma, bustling about in Grandma's kitchen while eight golden mounds of goodness puffed tiny tendrils of steam from the table.

"Why did you make pie, Mom?" At a very young age, I was thinking of all the work involved. I figured cake would have been a lot quicker, though cake mixes had not been invented back then.

"The men loved pie." She may have had visions of a slacker daughter. "And they worked so hard, they needed plenty of good food to keep them going." She described the heavy bundles of grain that the family had cut and tied to wait for the huge threshing machine. Grandpa had hired the owner whose strong horses pulled the contraption out to the field to "thresh" the kernels from the stalks. The neighbors came to help with the backbreaking work.

As Mom cut perfectly-spaced slits into the folded edges of the top crust on the board, she continued to share her memories: In a day or two, her dad and brothers would go to a neighbor's and help with their threshing. That farmer's wife would feed the men just like Grandma and her daughters. As I write this, I cannot help but wonder if this system motivated the wives to serve pies. After all, one would not want to be outdone by another cook; "Maude sure had good cherry pie!"

Our mother carried on the pie-making tradition for her own family. She took pride in giving her very best and made sure her own hard-working farmers were well fed. My sisters recall our older brother Donald grabbing a slice of apple pie from the counter and heading outside for morning chores— after a hearty breakfast!

So, this year, the day before Thanksgiving, I rolled, folded and patted. I peeled and sliced, covered and baked into golden goodness: apple and pumpkin. Thanksgiving morning the door opened and footsteps of various sizes padded into my kitchen. Suddenly, I was embraced in a hug, a bear hug by a much younger, though taller person. "Grandma, did you make pumpkin pie?"

I smiled. It just doesn't get any better than that!

Our mom baked many pies in this ceramic dish. Thank you Susan and Emily Nash for the photo.

Lemon Pie

Grated rind and juice of 1 lemon, 1 cup water
1 cup of sugar. boil together a few minutes.
One heaping tablespoon cornstarch dissolved
in a little cold water. beaten yolks of 2 eggs
added to syrup. boil until it thickens. Have
a crust pricked with a fork and baked. Turn
in filling. whip the egg whites, add 2 tablespoon
sugar. Spread on top. Set on upper grate to brown.

Banana Cream Pie

1 cup half & half 1 cup rich milk, yolks of 3 eggs,
2 tablespoon (heaping) of corn starch ½ cup
sugar, 1 or 2 bananas sliced. Put milk on to
boil, mix sugar, cornstarch and a pinch of salt
eggs yolks together with a little milk to make
a smooth paste. Pour into boiling milk mixture.
Cook. Pour half of mixture in a freshly baked pie
crust or graham cracker crust. add sliced bananas
Then rest of pie filling. And cover with meringue.

Raisin Pie

1 cup raisins, ½ cup water 1 cup cream (Sweet
or sour) 1 tablespoon flour, 1 cup sugar,
1 tablespoon Vinegar, 1 tablespoon cinnamon,
½ teaspoon allspice, ¼ teaspoon cloves 1 teas-
spoon Vanilla. Cook raisins in boiling water
for 5 minutes. Pour into it cream, sugar,
flour and other dry ingredients mixed. cook
until thick. remove from fire. Add Vanilla.
and Vinegar. Bake between 2 crusts.

Mom wrote down recipes she wanted to share with family.

35

13

Cooking Up Warm Memories

Most of my recipes require preheating the oven to a certain temperature before baking. As I start to mix the dough, I press two buttons in the top panel of my stove. The fire ignites. Within five minutes the appliance beeps to let me know it has reached the set temperature.

A few more steps were involved back when our mother fired up her cook stove more than 60 years ago. There were no switches, buttons or controls. First, she adjusted the draft on the chimney. Then she crushed a few sheets of newspaper and tucked them into the top part of the firebox which she had removed with the special handle that fit perfectly into the round burners. She added chunks of split wood and a few handfuls of corn cobs. She lit a match and held it to the paper to get the fire going. She replaced the top section of stove and the two heavy burners. Forty-five minutes later, Mom opened the oven door just a bit and stuck her hand in for a five-second temperature test. Cook stoves back then did not come with beepers because women came with built-in hand thermometers.

Our cook stove sat regally in the southeast corner of the kitchen. Two long handles and a "Monarch" insignia plate sparkled on the white enamel front. The top surface was a thick sheet of black cast iron. Mom and her daughters bustled around that huge metal box before meals and on baking days. The appliance also heated the kitchen and a good share of the house when north winds whirled.

It was the kids' job to keep plenty of fuel in the "cob box" next to the stove. At the end of the day, Donald or Delmer would carry in an armload of wood they had chopped. The girls took turns filling an aluminum tub with cobs from the pile left from corn shelling. Delmer was not very old when he used his "truck," the red wagon, to haul two wooden baskets of cobs.

Everyone in the family contributed in some way to the care and feeding of that old cook stove, but my siblings and I remember the delicious, warm feeling of home that came from it, especially in the weeks and days before Christmas.

Early in December, Mother assembled dried fruit, nuts, molasses and spices and blended them into a dark, rich batter for fruit cake. Citron, cinnamon and cloves permeated the air as the round cakes baked.

Our family of eight, plus guests and gifts required mass quantities of cookies to be stockpiled in giant glass jars and metal canisters. Each kind produced its own wonderful aroma as they reached golden perfection in the oven. There were soft molasses cookies and Mom's melt-in-your-mouth sugar cookies. The girls all helped make filled raisin wafers and salted peanut cookies. We frosted cut-outs and spooned jam into thumbprints. Delmer's favorite were chocolate chip. Mom never seemed to notice the drastic "settling" that occurred in that particular jar!

Our mother's Scandinavian heritage meant a family love for lefse. She mixed potatoes, butter, sugar and flour, then rolled pieces of the dough into thin rounds. My sisters carried them to the stove to bake—directly on top! Each puffed a mouthwatering potato-flour steam as it baked. My sisters flipped them over once and transferred to a plate when they were done. The lucky cooks got to eat the few that ended up with holes or crispy edges.

But times have changed. Today we bake lefse on special grills. I don't haul wood or cobs to fuel my gas range. A beeper replaced the cook's built-in hand thermometer.

My trusty stove still emits amazing aromas, especially close to Christmas, but nothing can compare to the memories of the old cook stove in the corner and all the ways it warmed us.

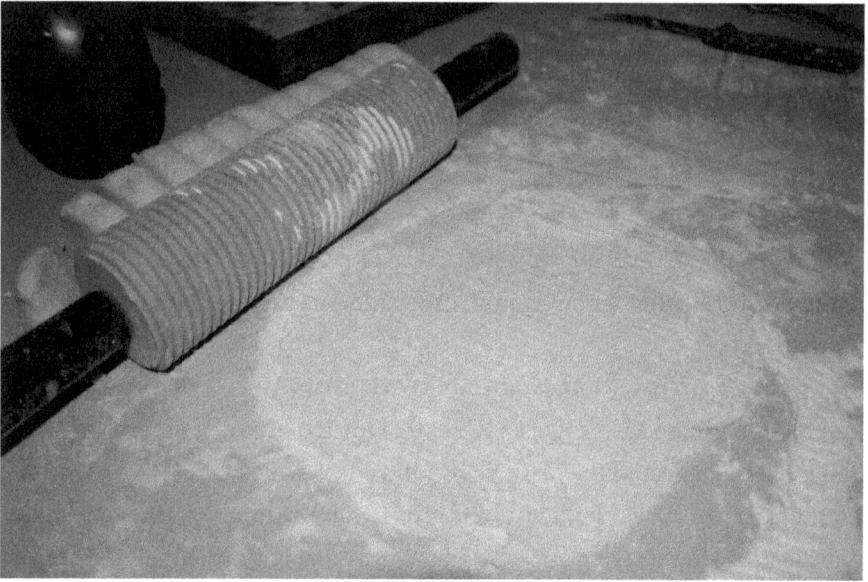

Lefse rolled out and ready to be baked on the griddle.

14

Hope Springs Eternal

The night is not quite silent. There is a soft gentle sound like tiny bells whispering a happy song meant only for the heart to hear. A shiny golden angel shimmers red to blue to green as she turns, reflecting the lights that are nestled around her. Under a canopy of stars, the angel's baton circles round and round, lightly tapping six hanging chimes. Clearly inscribed on the angel is the word, "HOPE."

The brass ornament, powered by a string of lights, calls to me every year from my Christmas tree. The sound, the sparkle and the continuous movement send a message as powerful as a hundred-voice choir: there is hope for the future.

Sometimes we have to look for it. Sometimes it shines as brightly as the sun on a cold winter's day. But always there is hope. Struggling small town newspapers keep printing pictures of high school sports heroes and little children talking to Santa. A group of volunteers devotes a huge share of time and resources to rescuing and finding homes for cats and dogs, simply because they love animals.

A community joins together to raise $40,000 with their Festival of Trees to help local organizations, including a church's shopping spree for kids. People pitch in when water damages their public library. Extension directors and staff and 4-H leaders selflessly give their time to educate and support youth in every positive endeavor.

One woman bakes hundreds of dozens of cookies and donates every penny to her local cancer fund. Volunteers support food and clothing pantries. A young man single-handedly raises money to build a monument for veterans. Youngsters and adults dig, plant, cultivate and harvest, working side-by-side to raise food for their town. The program is youth-inspired.

Scientists are working around the clock to develop better ways to prevent, diagnose and treat cancer. Studies are exploring new methods of fighting dementia. Plant biologists are exploring new plants that can produce more food, tolerate drought or absorb carbon dioxide from the atmosphere.

Caring people across the globe are working to cultivate compassion, encouraging all of us to broaden minds and open hearts. Often it is our younger generation which provides the impetus to build on common ground.

Some days I hate to admit it, but I don't see many reasons to be optimistic; hope is the last thing on my mind. There are times when I fear for our grandchildren and the world that we are handing to them. What will their future hold? Those are the times I need a reminder—the shiny little angel that keeps turning, keeps playing her soft, eternal song.

My wish for you this new year is a life full of gentle signs of hope that go on and on and on.

The angel continues to spread hope year after year.

15

The Heartbeat of Our Communities

"Step right up! Read all about it!" Do you remember the newspaper boys in the movies as they called out the latest breaking news? Headlines flashed on the screen. Presses churned out copies that spun in wild circles, with profound story titles announcing the end of the war, the destruction of the Hindenburg, the stock market crash. Newspapers have informed the public of world and local happenings since the invention of the printing press in 1440.

Atticus Finch read to his daughter Scout from "The Mobile Register" in *To Kill a Mockingbird,* highlighting the importance of reading and the father's dedication to keeping his child informed. Movie and television stars were often depicted with wire-rimmed spectacles riding low on their noses, holding large sheets of newsprint in front of them

Our father also stressed the value of keeping abreast of world and local happenings. He and Mom read the paper nearly every day. We would hear the rustle and see the printed pages held up before them as they scanned their favorite sections. Most often they read after supper in their easy chairs. Sometimes on less-busy winter days, they would sit at the kitchen table. I remember them discussing what they called "the funnies:" the misadventures of Blondie and Dagwood, the escapades of Dennis the Menace, Family Circus, Li'l Abner and Little Orphan Annie. The folks' talk piqued my curiosity and I began turning to the comics every day. I discovered Dick Tracey with his two-way wrist radio. Imagine that!

Mom enjoyed the women's pages and often cut out recipes. Both parents read "Ann Landers" and sometimes laughed at the quirky conundrums of her letter writers. The daily publication was not only a source of news, but also family entertainment. No matter what we read, my five siblings and I learned at a young age that we had better keep that paper in perfect order and folded neatly when we were finished. Dad did not appreciate re-sorting the pages!

Once a week, the mail man delivered *The De Smet News* to our mailbox. Almost always there was a story about someone we knew. Back then, people liked to read about social gatherings: who visited whom, birthdays and anniversaries, people in the hospital. School event photos often covered several pages. Mom would cut out stories and pictures that pertained to our family. In my tub of keepsakes, there is a manila envelope full of articles Mom saved for me. Articles about spelling contests and 4-H awards are mixed with obituaries of grandparents, aunts and uncles; they tell a life story.

Times have changed. We do different things for entertainment now than we did fifty years ago. People use different sources for information. The future of newspapers is uncertain. In some areas readership has declined. Postage has increased drastically. When businesses fold, advertising revenues dwindle. Smaller staff means less local news coverage. In the last twenty years, more than 2,000 small-town newspapers have closed.

Local journalism is the heartbeat of communities. Newspapers tell the story of the people and record it for future generations. They provide a place for dialogue. The information newspapers report is a binding force for communities, the eyes and ears of the public.

In the face of struggling publications, will parents still be able to clip stories of their children to tuck into their keepsake boxes? Will State Champs in 2040 be compared to those in 2025? Can we save our newspapers in spite of our changing world?

Several communities have taken steps to rescue their local newspapers, joining together with every possible resource to continue their publications. They made a difference. So can we. We can subscribe. We can buy copies.

Most importantly, we must keep reading. Like Atticus Finch, famous people of the past, and our parents, we must teach our children and grandchildren the love of reading and the need to be informed. Example is the most powerful teacher.

Wire-rimmed spectacles are optional.

16

Not Necessarily Necessary

Her freckled face burned bright red. She folded her hands, averted her eyes and whispered, "I need to use the necessary." This scene led to the attempted escape of the young woman from her captors in the historic novel I recently finished. If she could just get to the outhouse...

When our mother was growing up on her parents' South Dakota homestead, she trudged to the small wooden building in the back yard when nature called. On bitter winter nights there was a "chamber pot" available, but that had to be emptied. Yuk. Those were the only options. No indoor plumbing. No flushing.

During the first years of their marriage, our folks depended strictly on the little house out back. Deloris, Darlene and Dorothy remember having to take the 25-yard path to the privy. Going alone at night was scary for Dorothy; she begged Darlene to go with her. Flashlights didn't keep the terrifying night creatures away, but big sisters did!

Ours was built by the Works Progress Administration. The WPA was created by President Franklin Roosevelt to help bring the country out of the Great Depression by providing jobs for thousands of unemployed workers.

The bright white siding and black-shingled roof housed a cement floor that covered what needed to be covered. A small window close to the top allowed welcome light in the daytime. Inside were two seats, a big seat and a smaller seat. The holes on top also varied in size. Each seat had a wooden cover on hinges.

By the time Delmer and I came along, our parents had installed indoor plumbing. No more purposeful prances under the Milky Way. However, one important factor kept the path worn to the little white building—water. The water we used in the house for washing, bathing and flushing came from our cistern. The folks hired someone to haul water from De Smet to our front gate and pipe it into the cement reservoir. It took a lot of water for the family of eight, so we were encouraged to use the outside facility as often as possible. As the youngest, most spoiled in the family, I didn't mind. It was close to my tree swing and right next to the garden and Mom's clothesline. In the night I stayed cozy warm walking a few feet to the indoor bathroom.

At the time we didn't realize that little white building was teaching us valuable lessons:

We learned self-control. It was not smart to drink three cups of hot cocoa before bed.

We learned the Golden Rule; always be considerate of the next person. Sitting down only to discover an empty toilet paper roll was not fun.

We learned that lime was not always a fruit.

We learned how to speak in code. Even Mom smirked at Dad's after-lunch announcement: "I need to see a guy about a horse."

We learned that nothing should be wasted. Peach wrappers were soft and peachy-smelling. The Sears Roebuck catalog was for more than reading.

We learned to stop and smell the roses. Mom planted a yellow shrub rose a few yards from the facility. The flowers smelled wonderful on purposeful summer walks.

Today, few outhouses remain. To be honest, I try to avoid those that are necessary for use at crowded events or out-of-the-way sites. And I am truly relieved that most of the time such necessaries are no longer absolutely necessary!

17

When Overalls Could Stand

It's Monday morning. The sun is shining. Delmer informed me via text that it is five degrees in De Smet, South Dakota. On a similar January day nearly 70 years ago, our mother would have said, "It's a good day to get the laundry done."

The Maytag ringer-washer handled the washing part, but the amazing thing about winter laundry back then was how the clothes were dried. Barring snow showers or howling blizzards, Mom almost always hung the clothes out on the line. And Monday was almost always "wash day."

The first load was the whites, washed in good hot water. Bundled in winter coats and boots, I followed Mom out to the clothesline. She set her wooden apple basket down in the packed snow path. The canvas clothespin bag she had tucked into her basket came out first. She hooked it over the heavy wire and it worked in Goldilocks fashion (just right!), sliding along so the wooden clothespins were always just in her reach. Dish towels, hankies, whitey-tidies and bed sheets were soon clipped onto the icy line. I watched as they moved in the wind, flapping gently for a few seconds, then turning stiff and barely moving. Mom grinned as she saw the question in my eyes. "They'll freeze dry," she said.

Her hands had to be cold, but she kept on, working as quickly as freezing fingers allowed. Soon the basket was empty and we trudged back inside for the next batch. She did the same with the loads of colored clothing and finally the darks, the jeans and overalls.

There were three strong wires on our clothesline that were fastened on to three T-shaped wooden posts. Around fifteen feet of wire draped between each of the two sections. They ran parallel between the house and the yard fence. Some winters, the wind carved mountains of snow under the lines. The guys shoveled a wide path to clear the way. The clothesline was a critical part of life on the farm, especially before we got a clothes dryer. Fortunately, the same path led to the outhouse, which was also a critical part of farm life.

Darkness set in early on winter nights, so before chore time Mom headed out to bring in the clothes. All of my siblings remember helping. Frozen stiff, it wasn't like they would fluff back into the basket! Carefully extracting them from the clothespins and the wire, we carried in the bigger items like wooden boards in front of us. Our mother laughed as she stood a pair of Dad's striped overalls next to the cook stove to finish drying. Towels and aprons were laid on chairs or on a wooden drying rack.

It didn't take long for the cook stove to dry everything into softness, but in the meantime, the house was filled with the freshest, most amazing scent ever to be experienced by human noses—the smell of dried-in-fresh-cold-air laundry.

Others must have also appreciated the scent, for manufacturers have tried to emulate the heavenly fragrance. Candles, soaps, dryer sheets and detergents have ingredients that are supposed to remind us of those days of freeze-dried clothing. "Fresh Linen," "Clean Cotton," "April Fresh," "South Dakota Winter," (Sorry, I got carried away!) all try to imitate Mother Nature's powers.

They are not the same, but they do, however, conjure up a fun picture in my mind—a picture of Dad's striped overalls standing up all by themselves next to the kitchen stove.

18

One Good Egg Deserves Another

"It's so cold my chickens are layin' frozen eggs!" Buck and Roy told corny jokes between their guitar strumming refrains of Cripple Creek. It was called "Pickin' and Grinnin' and was a regular feature on the TV series *Hee Haw*. It's been pretty cold in Iowa, but I have yet to find a frozen egg this winter. I do remember occasionally finding one in our chicken coop when we were growing up. It had split open and I could see the frozen white part inside. Mom put it in a cup and poured cold water to thaw it. It was baked into the next batch of cookies. "Waste not, want not," Mom quoted. Buck and Roy and Mom remind me of old jokes, idioms, phrases and stories. I can't help but scratch up some more—about chickens!

My chickens seldom let an egg freeze because they suffer from empty nest syndrome. Yes sirree, Foghorn Leghorn! The girls in my coop have a hen party every time they decide to deposit their precious nest eggs. Goldie shimmies into the middle nest box. She preens and tucks in a wisp of soft down to feather the nest. Eventually, she plops out a big brown egg. In typical Mother Hen fashion, she sits on it a while and ponders the age-old question, "What came first, the chicken or the egg?"

Meanwhile, back in the coop, Mattie has a cackleberry about to drop and is thinking that Goldie is lollygagging. Heaven forbid that Mattie use one of the empty nests. She neglects Dad's sage advice: "Don't put all your eggs in one basket."

"She thinks she rules the roost!" Mattie clucks as she waddles, clinching more than her teeth. "I don't mean to ruffle your feathers, Goldie, but I'm walking on eggshells here!" Mattie is getting madder than a wet hen.

Counting her chickens before they are hatched, Goldie sits. At last, she stands, stretches, and stately struts off the nest. Mattie decides one good egg deserves another and rushes in to deposit her speckled brown egg next to Goldie's. The old biddy also remains on the eggs for a while. It is quite warm and cozy in the nest with three hen fruit snuggled beneath. She fantasizes about Rooster Cogburn. What's that? Had she said his name out loud? Dolly just popped her head in and tittered gleefully that Mattie had her stories scrambled. Then Dolly had the nerve to ask if Mattie was ever going to leave the nest. "You're no spring chicken, you know!"

"Well, if that doesn't just stick in your craw!" thought Mattie as she raised her hackles and glared at Dolly. Some hot chicks thought they were all that and a box of Chicken in a Biscuit. Mattie warmed the eggs a bit longer. Finally, she sauntered off the nest. With a cocky grin, she went eye-to-eye with Dolly and told her she walked like a roly-poly penguin! Then, as quick as you can say "sunny side up," Mattie flew the coop.

Now we know why the eggs don't freeze. All the girls lay in the same two nests. And they take their time doing it. Though some may seem a bit henpecked, they get along quite well, cackling happily because even on the most frigid days, they have something to crow about.

Chickens are also famous in children's literature, though the stories are not all they are cracked up to be. Chicken Little cried, "The sky is falling!" one too many times. I think dumb clucks are scarce as hens' teeth, but Chicken Little did end up with egg on her face.

Then there was the Little Red Hen. She woke up with the chickens. She took her children under her wing. She never chickened out. She free-ranged. She crossed the road. "Why?" you ask. To make you grin! Think of more common chicken sayings. If you can, the yolk's on me!

19

Saturday Night Lights

Some words were never, ever spoken at our house. We never said, "I'm bored." Our parents never said, "It's too cold for you to go outside." The folks stressed the value of exercise in the good old fresh air. As the youngest, most spoiled child, I stressed the value of hunkering down with a good book and dreaming of becoming a famous writer.

Delmer had other dreams and for a time during his growing up years, he aspired to be a quarterback like Johnny Unitas. My brother watched every televised football game, especially the Baltimore Colts, Unitas' team at the time. So, it did not come as a huge surprise one February night when Delmer strode into the nice warm kitchen with the football tucked under his arm. "Hey, DeAnn, let's go out and play catch. I need to work on my throwing arm."

I looked up from my book, *Trixie Beldon,* and frowned incredulously. I glanced at the window. "It's dark out."

"So? That's what yard lights are for. And the moon is even shining. It's a perfect night."

To be honest, I adored my older brother and usually enjoyed whatever adventures he contrived, but I didn't want him to know that. Visions of skating on Spirit Lake danced in my head while Delmer dropped his fishing line into a hole in the ice. I just needed to play my cards right. "It's like 20 below zero out there. We will freeze to death!"

"Oh, it isn't that cold. It's at least ten above. Come on, it'll be fun!"

I heaved the biggest sigh I could muster and reluctantly trudged to the porch to get my winter coat, boots and mittens.

We headed out into the yard. The packed snow reflected the light and it wasn't half bad out there.

I sort of jogged out to the Quonset to be in place. I figured I wouldn't catch anything anyway, so I wouldn't have as far to chase the balls.

"Good grief! Where are you going? Move up."

I rolled my eyes like every good little sister. "Unitas could throw that far!"

"Yeah, but he would have a receiver who could catch them." I couldn't argue with that.

An hour flew by quickly with Delmer throwing, me mostly missing and retrieving the balls. I would pick up the pigskin and run partly back to him and toss it. It wobbled and flopped and landed ten feet in front of him. "DeAnn, you need to learn to throw a spiral."

"Yeah, right," I said, trying really hard not to let my eyes light up.

He showed me where to place my hand on the ball, fingers between the white laces. "Then you flick your wrist like this when you throw and follow through with your arm."

I tried about 20 times and finally, a decent spiral soared right to my brother. "Good job! You did it!"

At last, we called it a night. Delmer went to check on the football scores. I went back to my book as though nothing exciting had happened in the last hour.

Monday morning, friends on the bus inquired about my weekend.

"Oh my gosh! It was so cool! Delmer and I played football Saturday night in the snow. There was just the yard light, but we could see just fine. He even taught me how to throw a spiral! And next weekend, I get to go ice skating on Spirit Lake!"

Delmer and DeAnn planning future football practice under the lights.

20

Through the Eyes of a Child

White starbursts, ferns and flowers sparkled gloriously on the kitchen window. Jack Frost had worked his magic. I pressed my hand into the crystalline masterpiece. The melted circle gave me a window to the outside world. Though it immediately began to cloud over, the sight before me took my breath away. Hills of white filled the front yard. Most were small mounds, but some were taller than I and curled at the top like a frozen ocean wave. The air seemed clear, but my eyes were drawn to movement over and around the snow-covered ground. Powdery wisps puffed and swirled, seemingly going on forever. The South Dakota blizzard had ended, but the snow drifted on.

The sound of shovel against wood invaded my winter wonderland. Donald and Delmer were scooping. Dad, Mom and the boys had gone out hours ago. Frozen tanks and pumps needed thawing. Mom's trusty teakettle had come to the rescue.

I was about to re-defrost my tiny porthole when Dad came in from the porch and deposited an armload of garments next to the chair by my window. He saw me and glanced at my peep hole. The serious look in his eyes flashed to a twinkle just for a second.

He sat on the wooden chair and began the cumbersome, but critical task of dressing for hours outside. He would be moving snow with the loader on the John Deere 730. There were no heated cabs back then. There were no cabs back then. Sitting at the controls, only his clothing protected him from the elements and the elements could be cruel. Forecasters predicted a high of minus two. The formula for wind chill factors was developed in 1945, but not used by the weather service until 1973. We never heard, "Today's wind chill will be fifty below zero. Stay inside."

Long Johns were standard farm equipment and Dad's peeked out from under his flannel shirt that he wore under his striped overalls. Thick wool socks stretched over the long underwear. He reached for his insulated coveralls and stepped down. Both feet in, he stood.

He did not speak or make any motion requesting help. But Mom was there at his side. She lifted the heavy shoulders of the coveralls up, first one side, then the other so that Dad could hold his sleeves down with his fingers while pushing his hands into the armholes. Mom did the same with the waffle-weave sweatshirt. He sat again and slid his Red Wing boots into his 5-buckle overshoes.

Mom found a stocking cap and scarf and thick leather mittens. She grinned as she pulled the stocking cap over his mostly-bald head and down to his eyes and put the hood up. He frowned at the scarf, but let her tie it over his face. There were liners in his yellow work gloves, but Mother still offered the mittens. "I don't know if I will be able to drive the tractor." He slid them into his pockets. Only his eyes were visible, but they met Mom's.

The guys spent the day moving snow. Yards, paths and roads were cleared. Livestock needed food, water and shelter. Mom and the girls kept the teakettle on the stove. Coffee, hot cocoa, sandwiches and cookies were ready when the workers needed to warm frozen fingers and toes.

At the end of the long, arctic day, the farmers trudged inside. Gloves, hats and scarves draped over chairs and hooks. Dad unbuckled his overshoes and set them on the designated newspaper. He stood. Again, Mom was there. She latched onto the sleeves of the sweatshirt and held on tight while Dad pulled out one arm, then the other. The same with the coveralls. Beethoven could not have orchestrated more perfectly. Dad gave Mom a peck on the cheek. After six children and twenty-some years of marriage, she still blushed.

Few words were spoken, but actions spoke volumes. Though I was only five, I saw much more than a farm wife helping her grateful husband with his coveralls. I saw a clear picture that will warm my heart forever. I saw love.

Mom and Dad

21

A Kid in the Candy Dish

I was alone in the house. Quite suddenly, I became really, really hungry for a piece of candy. Mom said when we got hungry for something, it probably meant that our body needed the nutrients in that food. Therefore, I was certain my body needed candy!

I pushed the stool over to the corner cupboard where Dad kept the candy dish. The steps pulled out from under the seat. I listened to make sure no one was coming in and climbed up the steps onto the counter. Dad pretty much controlled the candy dish. He had never said it was off limits to the kids, but some things were just understood. After meals sometimes he would bring the pretty container to the table and offer us a piece. He might encourage us with, "candy rots your teeth out." Then he would supposedly prove his point by removing his teeth. As if he ate a lot of candy growing up! During the Great Depression, I am sure candy was never on the grocery list. Was there even a grocery list?

The dish was clear glass, with ribs that extended from the center like spokes. A pointed handle on the cover begged to be lifted. I could see blurry red, yellow and white through the fluted glass. Checking again that I would not be caught in my covert candy surveillance, I lifted the cover. Three cellophane packages lay around the edges of a small stack of ribbon and filled candies left from Christmas. I only liked the filled kind with raspberry centers. They were all gone. The ribbon kind was too big to snitch. The bags were opened with tops folded over. Lemon drops, white peppermint lozenges and French burnt peanuts waited. The peppermint circles tasted like chalk in my opinion. The peanuts with the rough, hard coating were disgusting. I reached for the bag of lemon drops. The cellophane rattled like breaking glass as I pilfered one yellow drop. Likely, Dad would not notice a missing lemon drop.

I slid the dish back to its spot, quite disappointed that none of the treats were even close to my favorites. If my body needed candy to fill a nutritional deficiency, it would sure be nice to enjoy the takings. I started to wonder if Dad purposely chose the sweets he knew I didn't like, maybe to crunch my temptation to snoop in the candy dish. As the youngest, most spoiled child, this was difficult to swallow.

About to climb down, I noticed some bright colors hiding in the dark recesses. I reached back to reveal bags of circus peanuts, candied orange slices and red hots. Mom cooked the cinnamon-spiced red hots with apple slices to make candied apples, but I loved to just let the candy melt in my mouth. Far, far back was a white paper sack with wrapped peppermints, butterscotch disks and root beer barrels. I knew I would get busted if I opened the sealed bags, but at least there was hope for the future. Maybe no one would notice if I snitched one itty bitty root beer barrel. I was about to go for it when I heard the front door open.

I closed the cupboard, scrambled down the steps of the stool and rushed to put it in its place. Mom walked into the kitchen. I am pretty sure I had lemon-flavored guilt dripping from my quickly rotting teeth. She didn't seem to notice. She tied on her apron. "I'm hungry for baked apples. DeAnn, can you bring some apples from upstairs?"

I was suddenly hungry for baked apples, too. "Sure, Mom. Can we sprinkle red hots on top?"

22

Ice Storm Rescue

The sound woke her in the darkness. Rain pounded on the roof and sluiced down her bedroom window. The young girl wondered at the strangeness of rain in February, but soon drifted back to sleep.

Hours later, in the warm kitchen below, the rain still battered the north window. Deloris stirred the oatmeal on the cook stove while Mom sliced bread for toast. Dad and Donald were eating breakfast when the outside sounds shifted. The pounding grew louder, like hail crashing against the window and house. Almost as suddenly it stopped. An eerie silence seemed to blanket the house and the room darkened as a thickening layer of ice coated the window. Dad strode to the blurry frame and shook his head. He reached for his coat. "I need to check on the livestock." He told Mom not to go out, that he would do her chores.

Donald hurried for his own winter gear. Dad ruffled the boy's blonde hair. "You stay in for now, Son. I'm not sure what I will find, and don't want you getting hurt."

The little boy's shoulders slumped, for he always shadowed his father. Mom said he should get his tractor out. Deloris smiled when she heard "putt-putt" sounds coming out from under the table.

Soon Darlene and Dorothy awoke and Deloris helped Mom dress her little sisters and get their breakfast. The rain had stopped, but Deloris kept glancing at the coated window.

59

An hour later, the kitchen door flew open. Dad stepped in, worry etched in his frost-tinged face. "I need two big boxes."

Mom rushed to find what he needed. Her eyes met her husband's, but no words were spoken as he hurried out, boxes under his arm.

It seemed like forever to Deloris before she heard the stomping of boots through the porch and down the basement stairs.At last Dad peeked in the kitchen. "Want to come down and see what I found?"

Deloris and Donald sat on either side of their father. Mom and the little sisters huddled down behind them on the wooden steps. All eyes stared expectantly at the two boxes on the floor. Slight muffled sounds began, like something scraping on the bottom. Soon, a muted softness brushed against the insides, and a gentle tapping caused the top flaps to lift slightly. Deloris saw a bit of red, then the tip of a brown feather flash through the openings.

"Pheasants," Dad spoke quietly. "Eleven of them down by the haystack. I couldn't figure out why they weren't moving, so I picked one up. Her eyes and beak, her whole head and body was coated in ice. I don't think she could see me."

The noise from the boxes grew louder. Finally, Deloris wondered, "How come you didn't take them to the kitchen, next to the stove?"

"Well, I read somewhere that when humans get frostbite, they are to warm up slowly. Figured it might be similar for birds." Then his eyes twinkled. "And I didn't think your mother would appreciate chasing flying pheasants through her kitchen if they got out."

Deloris covered her mouth to stifle a giggle. Donald grinned. So did Mom.

When Dad was certain that feathers were dry, he carried the noisy boxes back out to the haystack. Deloris and Donald followed in his icy footprints. He opened the boxes and stepped back. The wild birds quickly rose into the air. Wings pounded and jubilant freedom calls echoed through the frosty stillness.

Deloris reached for her father's hand as they watched the pheasants glide over the trees in the pasture and disappear. "I'm glad you saved them, Dad."

Later that day the kitchen brightened as the sun melted the ice away. But my sister will never forget the covey of pheasants Dad rescued that wintry day and how they came to life in boxes in our basement.

Later years: Dad and Delmer

23

Fasteners to the Past

They clanked like rocks against the insides of the can as I swished my fingers through them. "I need a button for my spinner," I explained to Mom as I stared into the red and yellow Folger's coffee can with the ship on the front. At last, I found a large, flat black button with four holes in the center. I threaded my string through and tied a knot to form a circle. Soon the disk was whirling wildly in front of me as I stretched the string between my hands, alternately tightening and loosening as the button spun, making a lovely-to-a-kid twanging sound.

The old button container provided colorful, fun and useful materials for many projects. I stitched them on doll clothes. Mom used some to replace lost buttons on shirts and pajamas. The smaller circles were markers on Bingo cards. In my mind the can was simply the supplier of fun, useful objects.

That all changed one winter night as I sat on the floor at the foot of my mother's chair. She lifted a needle into the air, tugged slightly on the thread, then poked it back into the fabric. She was hemming a shirt for Dad. "DeAnn, go get the button can."

I fetched it. Mom quickly spotted a dark blue button. She asked me to find four more just like it. I stirred them around, examining the different disks from the top of the container. Not having any luck, I grabbed Dad's Argus Leader, spread it out in front of me and dumped out the buttons. The various objects shimmied softly into a tiny mountain.

At the very top teetered a small white duck. Bright red threads connected the two holes in the center. "Oh, how cute!"

Mom smiled. "I sewed those on a dress I made for Deloris when she was little. Darlene and Dorothy wore it, too." I dug through the mountain and spotted a lace-covered sphere with a wire shank on the back. "That might have been on Lilly's confirmation dress," Mom spoke softly, her needle paused for a moment.

I gazed at the lacy treasure and frowned. "Why would we have buttons from Aunt Lilly's clothes in our button box?"

"When I married your dad and left home, my mother gave me a whole can of buttons. We cut them off of old clothes, like you help me do now, and saved them. So, some of these are from when I grew up."

"Did Grandma get buttons from her mom, too?" My imagination suddenly became undone. Were some of these buttons attached to dresses that my great-grandmother wore on the ship from Sweden to America? Two pearlescent white circles gleamed together in the lamp light. Did Grandma Selma's mother lovingly fasten those very buttons on her baby's dress as the child lay in a makeshift crib in their sod shanty? The tiny buttons warmed my hand.

Strangely, a tarnished brass ball rolled over like a whisper. "Oh, Mom! What might this have fastened?"

She thought for a moment. "Maybe an old boot? My mother spoke of wearing them when she was young." Mom went on to tell how the boots laced with loops and round buttons. Button hooks were required to pull the clasp over each button.

As I pictured Grandma painstakingly hooking clasps over 20 round buttons every morning, a rough, metal circle, like one from a uniform, mysteriously sparkled from the pile. Did an uncle fight for his country, that button worn proudly upon his chest?

At last, five blue buttons waited on the arm of Mother's chair. I scooped up the rest and dropped them back in the can. Their sound was different somehow. No more harsh clunks. From that day forward, the buttons jingled like magical jewels whispering their songs, fastening me to those who made me what I am today.

24

Revenge of the Northern Pike

Our mother loved to fish. She loved catching them, cooking them, and eating them. I am pretty sure she did not mind the scaling and cleaning needed in the middle, either. Maybe it was because of her Scandinavian background. Or maybe it was because she almost always caught the most fish. Whether luck, skill or perseverance, if there were fish to be caught, Mom caught them.

If Dad merely mentioned going fishing, Mom would have sandwiches made, coffee in the thermos and the bait and tackle waiting by the door in twenty minutes. Time of year or temperature didn't matter. It was always a good day for fishing!

One cold February morning, Delmer and his young boys were driving by Mud Lake and decided to find out if the fish were biting. He turned off the Bancroft Road onto a rutted track that led directly onto the lake. Tires had worn a path over the frozen, snow-packed surface to a fairly smooth area on the north corner. Cars and pickups were parked at various angles, forming a village of vehicles.

Some people moved about carrying short fishing poles. A few cranked the bent-metal handle on ice augers, boring holes through the eighteen inches of ice to the unfrozen water below. If a fisherman or woman could find a previously dug hole, it might save a couple inches of drilling since those did not freeze clear up to the surface.

Delmer parked his pickup twenty yards from the group and the boys followed him to the ice anglers. They searched for familiar faces or vehicles and there on the northern edge of the lake, was the folks' green Crown Victoria. Mom sat on her fishing chair which was a five-gallon bucket, custom fitted with a cushioned cover. The car sheltered her from the wind. Blue eyes peeked out from under her stocking cap and parka hood. The toes of her five-buckle overshoes pointed to a hole in the ice. Her mittened hands held a short fiberglass pole, its line trailing to a small red bobber on the water. A matching bucket-chair waited a few feet away. Dad either preferred the social aspect of ice fishing or he was following Jesus' "fishers of men" commission.

Though only Mom's eyes and mouth were visible, they were all my brother needed to see. Mom's smile flashed brightly in greeting.

"Are they biting?" Delmer surveyed the area around the ice holes. A mound of slush was freezing at the rim of the opening. A long-handled, slotted dipper leaned against the minnow bucket, close to the car. Mom had used the dipper to scoop out the ice as it froze on the surface. Two striped perch flopped around behind her chair. Three more lay still, frozen. A bigger fish with a pointed nose flapped its tail; it's mouth still moved in the way of fish. A northern. Delmer stepped closer. Suddenly, his eyes were drawn to a bright red stain on the ice—a ten-inch circle. Blood? He glanced at the fish. All six of them would not have held that much blood. He frowned in concern. "What happened?"

Mom grinned. She held up her mittened left hand. "The northern got me when I was taking him off the hook." She glanced back at the culprit. Razor-sharp teeth gleamed from the fish's gasping mouth. Her blue eyes sparkled. "He'll taste really good."

"Are you alright?" Delmer's eyes searched the mitten. Wetness darkened the thumb part.

"Ya, I'm fine. Just a little cut." Grudgingly, she eased the mitten off. Dad's bandana, now soaked in blood, was tightly wrapped around her thumb. Just as she slid the mitten back on, her bobber wiggled and sank under the water. She grasped the rod and waited. Suddenly she jerked the pole up hard and stood to pull the line in. Soon another northern flopped on the ice.

Mom thanked her son for taking it off the hook, but assured him that she could handle it herself. She reached into the minnow bucket with her good hand and soon her bobber floated again.

Delmer still smiles as he remembers that long ago day on the frozen lake. Loss of blood did not hinder our mother, at least not when the fish were biting! She did love to fish.

Mom and her catch on the ice—this one a walleye. Thank you, Deloris, for the picture!

25

Sometimes Small Miracles are the Most Amazing

"I am so sorry." I pulled the heavy quilt over the stack of white boxes and tucked in the corners. "Thank you for all that you've given me." A brick on top, a bag of leaves and several two-by-sixes held the covering in place. My heart hurt as I felt pretty certain that this was good-bye to my faithful hive of honeybees.

It was mid-February. Up until then the winter had been fairly mild. Mild was about to end. The week's forecast showed daytime temps barely topping zero and nightly temps reaching twenty-five degrees below. I wondered how a group of tiny insects living in wooden boxes between frames of wax and honey could possibly survive such brutal conditions.

Each day I scoped out the small dark mountain. Did I dare hope? But forecasts only got worse. Snow fell one night, and the next day the quilt-topped mountain was capped with white.

Finally, after what seemed forever, the frozen inferno was over. I trudged through the snow and pulled the cover back from the front of the hive. I held my ear to one side and listened. Nothing.

Sunshine blazed down warming the next day to 55. Again, I trekked through the snow to check the bees. Within 30 feet, I noticed movement at the hive opening. I moved closer and gasped. The little critters were circling in front. I stood and watched a long time, for miracles are meant to be savored. Bees flew and returned, some whizzed by my ear. A gentle buzzing sound lifted in the breeze, nature's happy song of life.

The snow all around was pocked with little craters. A tiny brown spot centered each small basin and a light tan circle fanned around the spot and faded to white at the crater's rim. There were hundreds of these little indentations, each a result of a bee's cleansing flight and the warming sun. Never wanting to soil their hives, the critters hold their poop all winter until the first balmy day.

As I observed, I remembered our father telling of helping his dad with bees. During the Depression they drove around to neighboring farms, trying to sell the syrup cans of honey they had collected. Did Dad's memories plant a seed in the heart of his ten-year-old daughter? I only know I dreamed of having bees someday.

Over the years, I have learned much of the science of what takes place in a bee hive, but I decided to find out exactly how those awe-inspiring, fuzzy girls had survived such a prolonged bitter spell.

Simply put, honey bees must create their own heat source and be able to reach a food supply (stored honey) in order to survive cold. The queen needs a temperature of at least 80 and is protected at all cost. Once temperatures fall to 57 in the hive, workers begin to form a cluster around the queen and younger bees. As the hive cools to 23, the bees in the cluster squeeze together tightly, rapidly vibrating their muscles to generate heat. They keep their heads pointed inward. This moves the heat to the center, allowing the bees in the middle to feed on honey. The outer shell of bees remains nearly motionless, acting as insulation. The inner bees, who continuously vibrate their wings trade places with the outer bees so they can warm up. The cluster expands and contracts as the temperature fluctuates, keeping that core temperature near 80 degrees. All the time, there is a constant insulating, vibrating, feeding, and switching places while they slowly position themselves over a fresh supply of honey.

Scientists theorize that some bees are strangely able to warm their own bodies to provide a heat source. Infrared images of study hives show tiny oval-shaped hot spots close to the hive center. How can these select few insects become little heaters?

Turns out no one knows. That makes it even more amazing!

Checking the small miracles with Grandson Jackson.

26

The Corn Has Ears!

"Why shouldn't you tell secrets in a cornfield? Because the corn has ears!"

Possibly the riddle was the source of our mother's code words of caution; she would say something similar when we kids were in the presence of adults and "questionable" topics entered the conversation. Some things were not discussed in front of children.

One March afternoon I sat next to Mom at the oil-cloth-covered table at Grandma's house. A spoon-filled glass, a covered butter dish, a sugar bowl, glass salt and pepper shakers, and a container of rusks served as permanent centerpieces. Grandma had mixed a glass of Tang for me. The adults, including two uncles, dipped the dry crisp bread (Skorpor) in their coffee. I bit into one of the rusks and the neighbors two miles away likely heard the crunch. The adults laughed. "Give that girl some coffee!" an uncle suggested.

"Nah, it will stunt her growth," Grandma stated seriously.

The adults laughed and the conversation turned to local happenings. I listened (and crunched), enjoying the adult dialog, something about someone losing their farm. All at once Mom cut in. "There are ears in the cornfield." A second or two of silence ensued. Grandma suddenly asked about the price of eggs from the egg truck. At the time I was quite baffled as to the relevance of eggs to the cornfield and a bit disappointed that I didn't learn the end of the story of the poor farmer. But children were to be seen and not heard, at least at Grandma's house, so I dipped my rusk in the Tang and chewed more quietly.

A few months later, three of Mom's sisters, Lilly, Julia and Ida, sat around our kitchen table. Mom served coffee and cake. I loved listening to my aunts. They often reminisced of the past. Their stories painted pictures of their youth and how different my mom's life was from mine. Blue eyes sparkled as the women chattered on. Julia delved into a story I was beginning to enjoy immensely when suddenly the tale transposed to Swedish! I frowned, disappointed at missing the rest of the story, especially when it ended with the four shaking in laughter, and tears of mirth pouring down their faces.

Later, I asked Mom about the story. "You are too young," Then I asked her if she would teach me Swedish.

The folks believed that some topics were not for youngsters' ears. Finances, neighbors' misfortunes, miscarriage and pregnancy were not discussed when my siblings and I were around. Back then couples did not announce upcoming births until said event was quite obvious in spite of loose-fitting dress.

Occasionally, Delmer and I would be comfortably seated in the living room, Mom and Dad in their easy chairs, when "Gunsmoke" flashed on the black and white screen before us. If the opening scene was a wild shoot-out chase of the bad guys, Dad might instruct his "remote" (me) to change the channel. "Kids don't need to be seeing that violence." (The remote walked very slowly.)

Often when readers comment about my stories, they say "Those were the good old days." Or "Those were simpler times."

Reflecting, I am not sure I agree. I still wonder what Mom and her sisters thought was so funny that day. As for "simpler," maybe. I would say "quieter." After all, not only did the corn have ears, the potatoes had eyes and the celery would stalk you!

Two of Mom's sisters: Julia and Lilly

Aunts Lilly, Julia and Ida. Confirmation photo.

CANDLES AND MIRRORS

27

Melting Mountain Memories

All that remained was a four-foot oval of gravel in my front yard. Two weeks ago, those rocks were hidden in a pile of snow, the result of clearing my drive after a storm. The white mound shrank in the sun, exposing the stones. Strange how something so mundane can awaken a childhood memory:

The South Dakota blizzard had raged for two days, leaving hip-high drifts in its wake. Dad and my brothers began the arduous task of clearing the snow to allow access to the buildings and livestock. I stared through the kitchen window as Dad maneuvered the John Deere 730. He lowered the front-end loader and drove into a drift. The harsh scraping sound of metal on gravel vibrated into the house. He lifted the scoop, steered to an area just off the driveway and dumped the snow. The pile grew taller and I imagined Dad building that enormous white mountain just for me!

Mom came in from chores as I was pulling on my gray wool snow pants. "You stay close to the house until Dad gets done moving the snow." As the youngest, most spoiled child, I seldom had stern orders, but Mom was serious this time. I headed outside and waited inside the gate. Finally, with a wave and a smile, Dad chugged by to the barnyard. It was safe to explore my snow mountain.

I fetched sleds and scoped out the pile. It was important to scale Mt. Everest on the best side for scaling and avoid making tracks on the good sledding side. My boots sank deep into the snow, so I abandoned the sleds and stomped to make toe-holds or rough steps all the way to the top. There I stood.

My brother stepped out of the barn and I yelled, "Hey Delmer! Come sled with me!" He grinned, but I knew he would finish chores first.

I half-stumbled, half-slid back down to the sleds. My favorite was the wooden one on thin metal runners. The crossbar on the front with the rope attached on both sides gave me a sense of control. But my vast sledding experience (I was seven, after all.) had taught me that likely those runners would sink in, sending me tumbling. So, I pulled the blue saucer to the summit, sat down and pushed forward, tightly gripping the sides. The disc propelled downward, spinning all the way. Most youngsters likely reveled in all that action, but I preferred straightforward movement. So, after five or six dizzying, trail-packing rides, I decided to try the wooden sled.

It teetered on the peak as I stepped across to straddle, then eased down and carefully tucked one boot into the opening by the crossbar, then the other. I leaned forward and began the descent. The sled picked up speed and I flew down, screaming all the way. Inertia carried me on far beyond the slope, and I stopped short of the straw pile before the barn.

Soon Delmer climbed the mountain. Of course, his first try took him all the way to the straw pile. "You only made it that far because I packed the trail first!" I hollered at his whoop of triumph.

I trudged to the house to ask Mom for a box. First, we tried sitting in it, but it tipped. We flattened it and Delmer plopped on and whirled down, his body bouncing as the cardboard flexed into crevices.

I noticed Dad watching from the gate, leaning on a shovel. Soon, he was standing by the mountain, hazel eyes twinkling. My brother and I followed our father to the top, shovel at his side. He positioned the blade under him, the handle pointing forward at an upward angle. He shot us a grin, and suddenly began charging down the hill. His knees bent so his boots fit on the shovel curve. He leaned back to level the shovel on the slope. Almost to the bottom, the shovel twisted and Dad flew off. I held my breath as he landed, rolled and jumped to his feet in an instant. I wondered how such an old guy could be so agile? He was getting close to fifty!

Soon, tired but content, we tucked all the "sleds" into the front yard for the night.

Today, a few small pebbles remain in an oval on my lawn, the rake evaders. The rest are back on the driveway. The mound melted into the earth, but my childhood memories of sledding down our snow mountain endure forever.

28

Know When to Run

My lungs burned like fire and my heart pounded wildly. Behind me, footsteps bit into the gravel, but I pushed on. He was getting closer! At last, I reached the gate, slipped through and jerked it shut behind me. Chest heaving, I whirled to face my pursuer. One beady eye stared up at me for a second. Then he pecked at something on the ground and strolled nonchalantly back to the barn.

For one summer I lived in fear of the banty rooster on our farm. His tail curled with blue and purple plumes. Iridescent feathers collared his proud head like a lion's mane. They puffed up when he was angry, revealing a thin bare neck. But what scared me most were his spurs—little swords attached to each foot.

Dad told me not to run. "If you face him without fear, he will walk away." Easy for Dad to say. At five, I was much closer to the ground.

So, as an adult, I resolved that I would never again live in fear of a rooster. If one so much as looked at me cross-eyed, it was to the soup-pot with him.

Brooster came into my life as one of six baby chicks. Of course, I didn't know he was a rooster until he was old enough to crow. I had read that a rooster will protect the flock from predators, so I decided I would keep him, as long as he behaved.

Life was good and the hens were happy until one afternoon, as I was carrying the water bucket from the coop, something rammed into my back legs. I whirled around to see Brooster scurrying away. Two bruises centered with small punctures reminded me of my rooster's transgression for several days. But I could not bring myself to get rid of him. (Sometimes soup-pots are over-rated.)

I decided to try to make him a pet. Surely, he would not attack if he learned to like me. Every night I grabbed him off the roost, held him on my lap (tightly grasping spurry feet) and petted him. I explained that he could stay if he was a good boy. Every night he glared at me with a beady eye that told me I did not know how to make friends and influence roosters. I gave up on the best-buds plan, but learned to cope with having a mean rooster. I never turned my back when he was close by. I always wore long pants and boots. It worked, mostly, and years went by as Brooster's spurs grew to four inches. I still kept a wary eye behind me.

One day last fall, the old rooster had his chance for redemption. The flock was outside, searching for bugs. I was working in the garden not far away. All at once, Brooster crowed out a frantic alarm. The hens scurried to shelter. I cautiously scoped the yard, wondering what danger lurked in the shadows.

Suddenly I spotted movement. A tawny-gray shape skulked toward Brooster. A coyote! I yelled and headed for that wily critter, running right past Brooster. The coyote hightailed back into the woods, never to be seen again.

The event established a truce between Brooster and me. He never attacked again. Did he admire my bravery at taking on the coyote? Or, did he know that if I had not intervened, he likely would have given his life for the flock?

Anthropomorphism is the term for giving human characteristics to animals. I find it easy to do, especially when I have grown to love the creatures.

Brooster died yesterday. His age-worn body now rests under an aronia tree, close to the spot where he stood, ready to fight the coyote.

I will miss the feisty old guy who taught me that I could love even a mean rooster. I also learned when to run.

Brooster, my mean rooster

29

Heads Up to the Farmer's Wave

He tucked his billfold in the back pocket of his striped overalls and reached for a clean cap from the hook behind the door. "I need to run to town for a part for the planter." Dad spoke to Mom.

I gazed up at him with my best puppy-eyed-please-take-me-with-you-look. His hazel eyes twinkled. "Want to ride along?"

Never did I turn down the chance to shadow my father. Whether to town or to check for baby calves in the pasture, I was ready to tag along. On this sunny spring day, I wrestled with the door handle with both hands and crawled into the 1954 blue-gray Ford pickup. Dad's foot pressed the round rubber clutch pedal as he turned the key and pressed a button on the dash. He let up the clutch and pressed the gas pedal and we were off.

Short legs sticking out in front of me, I stretched my neck to see out the window. There were no seat belts in those days. Dad rolled his window down with the crank on his left and rested his elbow on the open frame. My side squeaked as I tugged on the handle. The "air conditioner" buffeted our faces as we turned onto the gravel road to De Smet.

Oncoming traffic was rare on those gravel roads, but that day a vehicle approached. Dad pulled to the right on the loose gravel to allow room to meet. As the pickup drew close, I saw the index finger on Dad's right hand lift. The man in the other vehicle proffered the same greeting. "Who was that?" I asked as the vehicle disappeared in a cloud of dust behind us.

"I don't know, but he was friendly." Dad smiled and focused on the fields and pastures as they slipped by. In another mile, a car turned onto the road ahead of us off highway 25. This time the other guy waved first, lifting two fingers, slightly bent. Dad returned the greeting.

On the blacktop we met more vehicles, and every driver waved, nodded or smiled, extending some sort of cordial greeting.

We traveled through town and on to the John Deere Implement business. I followed Dad inside. A man greeted him by name and they shook hands. The man smiled at me. "Hello, young lady." I answered politely and the men spent ten minutes discussing the weather, moisture in the soil and planting progress. I admired the tiny green tractors on the counter, Dad paid for the repair part and we were soon on the road again, meeting and greeting.

The "farmer's wave" came up recently in a conversation with some of my peers. "Nobody does that anymore," was the consensus. I shook my head. I refused to believe that this gesture that instilled in me as a child a sense of belonging, respect and trust has totally vanished. So, I decided to do my own research.

The next day I headed to Missouri Valley with the intention of testing out friendly-driver sign language. The first vehicle I met was stopped at the crossroads. Her head was bent down, obviously engaged. I drove on. A pickup approached. I was ready, having decided to use several fingers so my gesture would not be misconstrued as a different single finger wave. I waited for the right moment, lifted my hand and looked for the other driver's face. I frowned. Like the woman at the corner, this person was staring down in front of his steering wheel. A car approached from the curve ahead. This encounter would surely be positive. My hand was ready to lift in greeting when the vehicle crossed the center-line! I grasped the wheel and swerved to avoid collision. The driver pulled back into his lane, but he never even looked up.

Does the farmer's wave, this simple gesture of human kindness, no longer exist in a world that needs it the most?

I decided to try my experiment again, seeking some small glimmer of hope. This time I waved and smiled at the woman I met as we crossed the railroad tracks. She smiled and waved back with her whole hand. The best part was: she was looking up!

30

Patently Stretching the Truth

It sparkled in the light like a clear diamond facing the sun. I stared, mouth agape. It rested on a box, just at my eye level. A half-inch strap on top fit into a heart-shaped, jewel-studded buckle on the side. A brown rubber heel and sole peeked from the bottom. But the best, most amazing thing about the shoe was the clear, shiny covering on the white surface. I gazed at it, knowing its mate waited inside the box. I imagined my feet snuggled in sparkle, like Cinderella's glass slippers. I HAD to have them.

"Mom, come see these shoes!" I forced my eyes away for just a second to Mother, who was browsing nearby in the department store. "They would be really cute with my Easter dress." I began the spiel before she could even open her mouth. "Please, Mom, can we buy them?"

She didn't grab the box and head for checkout, but she didn't say "no" either. "Well, I suppose you could try them on."

As she looked up, a clerk approached with a smile. "Does the young lady need shoes today?" Mom politely asked the man if I could try them on. She told him my size and he strode off. I sat on a chair with a short, angled stool in front of it. My heart pounded with excitement. Finally, he came from the back room, carrying two identical boxes. He shook his head. "I'm sorry, but we are all out of that size. I brought the two closest sizes; possibly they will fit?"

"We'll try the bigger one first," Mom sat across from me as the man gently removed the shoes from the tissue. He slipped them on over my anklets and adjusted the buckle. I stood. A quarter-inch opening gaped above my toes and at the back.

The salesman placed those back in the box and glanced at Mom as he unwrapped the smaller pair. I wanted them to fit so badly. The new-leather smell filled my senses and made those shoes even more wonderful. Straps open, I pushed my right foot into a waiting shoe, then my left. My Cinderella dreams pinched a bit, but I was determined to make them fit.

Mom frowned a little and pushed down on a toe with her thumb. "Are they too tight?"

The gems sparkled up at me from the buckles. The shiny clear coating gleamed in the light. "They fit," I said without looking at Mom. I took a few steps and twirled around to assure her.

She was quiet for a few seconds, but finally told the man we would take them. I was so excited. I couldn't wait for Easter. I would wear my new pink, flower-flocked dress and my wonderful new shiny shoes!

Mom bought a pair of thin nylon anklets, and on Easter morning, I carefully pulled them over my feet and folded down the lace-topped cuff. With a happy sigh, I stepped into my new shoes. My toes scrunched inside, but sometimes a girl has to sacrifice in the name of fashion. In church, I kept swinging my legs up so I could admire my shoes. AND they felt more comfortable when I was sitting.

Two Sundays later, when I took those patent-leather wonders out of the closet, I could not force my feet in. My tummy hurt, but I found my school shoes and slipped them on instead. I am sure my mother noticed the absence of my beloved glass slippers, but she never said a word.

Reflecting, I wonder if Mom knew all along what was going to happen. Likely, she figured those patent leather shoes would teach her youngest child an important lesson. Likely, she was right.

31

I Don't Know Why You Say Goodbye I Say Hello

"Come here, I want to see you!" The directive was the very first phone call made by Alexander Graham Bell to his assistant, Thomas Watson. The call was made on March 10, 1876. Bell was experimenting with the "telephone" in his lab in Boston and succeeded in transmitting the words to Watson, who was on a different floor of the building. The event marked a pivotal moment in communication history, using wires to transmit speech.

The invention caught on, though the first systems required operators to connect the calls. On "The Andy Griffith Show" Sarah, the telephone switchboard operator, was mentioned 23 times but she was never seen. Andy cranked the handle on the wall set, held a device on a cord to his ear and spoke into a sort of microphone on the wall. "Sarah, give me…" Silent Sarah connected the call.

Dial forward a few decades to our growing up years on the farm. Thousands of telephone poles and miles of copper wire linked our country from coast to coast, allowing almost immediate voice to voice contact. A shiny black phone rested on a small cabinet in our kitchen. The handle contained both the speaker and receiver, conveniently connecting one's ear and mouth while being held in the center with one hand. We used the rotary dial to indicate the number we wished to contact. The handle was connected to the base and the base was connected to a wire in the wall. Any long conversations required pulling up a chair. Our farm joined several neighbors on a "party line," adding drama and frustration to life, but that's another story!

The folks discouraged long, unnecessary conversations. Calls outside the Erwin and De Smet area were long distance, which meant our phone bill included each with a per-minute charge. There had to be a really good reason for every one of those calls.

My sisters recall the pay phone in the lobby of their college dorms. Whether they called home or boyfriends, they needed a good supply of change to feed into the phone for every few minutes of talk time.

Collect calls, also called reversing charge calls, could be made from distant phones or pay phones through the operator. (Dial 0.) She then called the receiving party, asking if they would accept the charges. These were even more expensive than long distance, but Mom and Dad assured us that if we ever got in a predicament where we needed to contact them and had no other means, we should call collect.

For a few more decades, lines of communication opened. People could contact family, friends, businesses, which allowed more and better face-to-face connections. We let our fingers do the walking. No more being isolated during long winters on the farm. It was fun to say "hello."

In no time at all, new technology brought about new phones that did not need wires or cords. These new devices fit in pockets and purses. They can call or send messages instantly; cost is covered by a monthly plan. Smartphones can take pictures and send them to others. They will answer our questions. No worries about feeding in money or running up fees. This age of communication we live in is totally amazing. Or is it?

Some busy parents tuck in little ones with a phone. "Play your game until you get tired." Laps are being replaced by apps. Will bedtime stories become obsolete?

There are questions about who really invented the phone. Want to learn more? We could visit our libraries, go to the history section and study. Good for libraries. Good for our brains. Or we can just ask our phones.

We no longer need to store phone numbers in our memories, an excellent brain exercise. We can simply say, "Call Dorothy" or push a button. Do you ever have to look up your own number? I do.

Sitting in a restaurant where people should be talking, laughing, enjoying social interaction, I hear silence. Phones are lit up next to plates. Can people still communicate, one-on-one, face-to-face? Is it irony that Bell told Watson, "I want to see you."

Yes, Mr. Bell, your invention changed how the world communicates, but is it also changing us?

32

Warm Fuzzy Memories

Have you ever had a flashback that is so amazingly clear that you see that moment in time as though it just happened? Every one of your senses joins in the remembering and you can actually feel the same emotions you felt so long ago?

The door of the school bus creaked and thudded shut behind me. I stomped through the gray slush, loving the way it splashed away from my boots and left giant tracks in what was left of the South Dakota winter.

"Hurry and change your clothes. I have something to show you." Mom greeted mc as I stepped in the kitchen door, her smile sparkling in her gentle blue eyes. In less than five minutes, I was back downstairs. We bundled into our chore clothes and headed outside.

Past the windmill and granaries, we approached the white, windowed building that faced south, the brooder house. My heart pounded with excitement as Mom slowly opened the wooden door. For just a second, I heard a happy blend of soft peeping and tiny foot pattering. But the melody halted abruptly. Fifty little yellow heads waited at attention when they heard the sound of humans. We stood quietly in the warmth for a bit while they decided we were not a threat. One little chick pattered across the cardboard Mom had placed on the floor under the three heat lamps. Instantly, five more joined the party and soon the entire group resumed their activities.

Straw bales on their sides partitioned the area and provided spectator seating. The smell of straw blended with a medicinal odor that reminded me of the red liquid Mom applied to our cuts with a glass wand.

Pieces of cardboard rounded out the room corners. Mom said they prevented the babies from piling on top of each other if they got scared. Under one lamp a big glass jar sat upside down on a wide, red plastic dish. Several little yellow beaks dipped into the water and lifted their heads to swallow. I heard a bubble rise in the jar as more water gurgled down into the dish.

Two narrow metal feeders were also tucked in the radiant heat spots. A fluted bar stretched from end to end on top of each feeder. The bar twirled as a chick tried climbing over it. I giggled as she tumbled over the side, almost forgetting I needed to be quiet. "What is that bar for?" I whispered to Mom.

"It keeps them from scratching out the food, and pooping in it." I heard Mother's soft chuckle. We sat and watched for a long time, simply enjoying the antics of new babies, thrilled to be alive.

Finally, Mom stood and very carefully stepped over a bale. She waited patiently near a feeder, then bent slowly, reached down and encircled a chick with long, gentle fingers. She turned to me and settled the little one into my hands.

Then she caught another baby and we both sat, holding the tiny balls of fluff. Next to us, small creatures peeped softly, tiny feet pattered and scratched. Some chicks nodded to sleep in the warm light of the heat lamps, feet stretching out behind them.

I cradled the warm fuzzy creature under my chin and stroked her soft downy head with one finger. She snuggled in and closed her eyes. Mom smiled. Time stood still while it etched a forever picture in my mind.

This morning, I held one of my new baby chicks, cradling her next to my heart. I stroked her soft head. She closed her eyes. Suddenly I was ten years old, sitting next to Mom on the straw bale in the brooder house. She was smiling.

One of this year's baby chicks making warm, fuzzy memories with granddaughter Kylie.

Younger granddaughter Josie. Chickens need kisses too!

33

The Gadget That Altered the World from the Living Room

"No good will come of this device." British journalist C. P. Scott is believed to have made the prediction about the initial invention of the television. Mr. Scott was referring to the etymology of the word, a combination of Greek and Latin, but now we know the rest of the story.

Around 1884, European masterminds came up with a means of adding pictures to sound and transmitting the results. It took more than ten years for the first TV set to be created and marketed. Even then, it was seen as a novelty with only around 50 people owning one. In spite of a limited audience, the British broadcasted the Berlin Summer Olympic games in 1936.

Meanwhile, in the United States, the technology was also growing. At the 1939 World's Fair in New York, RCA unveiled the first publicly accessible television broadcast in America. It showcased President Franklin Roosevelt's speech for the opening ceremony. Television sets went on sale to the public the very next day. RCA/NBC began regular broadcasting.

Pearl Harbor became the first major news story announced by television. WWII slowed the growth of the product, but it made up time after the war. Television became established in American life. The World Series was telecast in 1947. By July of 1948, there are 350,000 TV sets in the USA.

By 1955 a Zenith console held a place of honor in our farmhouse living room. The contraption was nearly three feet wide and 20 inches deep. Encased in a mahogany-stained wood box on legs, the curved-front glass screen was around 22 inches wide. There were two round knobs on the side to adjust volume and select the station. The station handle clicked on each number. There were thirteen potential stations on the dial, but even though Dad had stationed an antenna on a pole behind the house, we received only three or four channels. Sometimes those were not very clear. Adjustment was necessary when the picture kept slipping up, up and away, or lines and static caused frustration for those of us anticipating our favorite programs.

Shows that aired in 1960 included "Gunsmoke," "Wagon Train," "Have Gun – Will Travel," "The Andy Griffith Show," "Meet the Press," "Howdy Doody," "Candid Camera," "The Ed Sullivan Show" and "The Real McCoys." "Captain 11," produced in Sioux Falls, was popular with the after-school crowd. As a youngster, I enjoyed just about all of them.

There was no remote and our father was the sovereign ruler of the picture box. Occasionally, he felt a western was "too violent for kids," and ordered one of us to change the channel. When the folks weren't home, we enjoyed the freedom of watching what we wanted. Chores, supper, dishes and homework were finished in record time!

Years later, as an adult, especially as a parent and a librarian, I have moments when I wonder if Mr. Scott was right. I have questioned program content. I have seen TV used as a babysitter, a substitute for human interaction. Have we lost communication skills when a large portion of our time is spent staring at a screen?

Does all that sitting contribute to a sedentary lifestyle, which leads to health issues? Do imaginations even work anymore when the picture instantly flashes before us? Would reading or other creative endeavors be better for our brains? Would our time be better spent outside? Is our dependence on entertainment technology causing us to lose touch with the wonder and beauty of nature? It is something to consider.

But I have fond memories of the family gathering in front of the set as the theme music blared. Crunching Mom's buttered popcorn while watching the good guys win. Laughing at Lucy. Looking forward to next week's episodes.

No, Mr. Scott, I believe good came of that ingenious invention and still does today. How much good and how to use it is up to us.

DeAnn in front of our first television.

34

You've Got to Stand for Something or You'll Fall for Anything

"A little dab'll do ya!" The cartoon guy's hair magically morphed from shaggy to shiny. The announcer claimed that when you use it, the girls will love to run their fingers through your hair. Background singers crooned in barbershop harmony, "Brylcreem, Brylcreem, Brylcreem."

Dad ran his hand over the top of his shiny bald head. "Maybe I should get some of that." Mom and the kids laughed as we sat in front of the television one Saturday night. Dad was always a good sport about his lack of hair and we were used to the tinny-sounding ads that often interrupted the best parts of shows.

The use of television advertising began in 1941 when Bulova ran a plug before a Brooklyn Dodgers game. The ad cost $7.00. It promoted watches. It lasted ten seconds. Those ten seconds changed America forever.

By the time our family was enjoying good old black and white television some 15 years later, an ad lasted close to a minute and there were about ten inserted throughout an hour-long show. But quite often, the commercials were as enticing as the programs. Likely, we sat entranced as the catchy ads promoted toys, beauty products, food, gum, soft drinks, and much more.

My siblings and I remember many of the same ones: "Folger's coffee. Good to the last drop." "Snap, crackle, pop! Rice Krispies!" "You wonder where the yellow went when you brush your teeth with Pepsodent." "Ring around the collar!"

Famous singers of the time promoted with song: "See the USA in your Chevrolet..." "You can trust your car to the man who wears the star." "Nothin' says lovin' like something from the oven and Pillsbury says it best!"

Prime-time ads sometimes appealed to children. "Oh, I wish I were an Oscar Mayer wiener." "I am stuck on Band aid 'cuz Band aid stuck on me!"

Some implied that if you used their product, you would instantly transform into the most popular, sexiest person on earth, free from bad breath or body odor. "You've got a lot to live and Pepsi's got a lot to give." "People who like people like Dial. Don't you wish everybody did?" Then there was the men's cologne ad in which the guy was literally fighting off women with his martial arts moves—"Hai Karate—drives women out of their minds."

The silly ones stick in our minds. "How about a nice Hawaiian Punch?" "I can't believe I ate the whole thing." "When it says Libby's, Libby's, Libby's on the label, label label..." Then there was Mr. Whipple's catchphrase: "Please don't squeeze the Charmin!"

Our father noticed that his children were rather enthralled with those tempting ads. He was concerned that we might be gullible enough to succumb, so he educated us in the psychology of commercialism. "The company wants to sell their product, but it's no better than any other brand...Mom's cookies are way better than boughten...one soap is as good as another. People don't need that stuff, but those advertisers try to make us think we do."

So, we were tough and strong (like Mr. Clean!) and armed with knowledge. We knew what those conniving advertisers were up to, and we would stand strong and not fall for their shenanigans.

Dad drove a Ford. We seldom bought cookies, but if we did, they were not the more expensive brands. Home canned vegetables served the purpose. Mom allowed root beer for floats and 7-Up for settling tummies; that was the extent of our "pop" purchases. Cheaper bandages covered cuts. Scrubbing stopped ring around the collar.

No sirree! We would never fall for those advertising gimmicks! It was just a coincidence that eventually Mom preferred Folger's coffee. Rice Krispies sometimes graced our breakfast table. Dial soap rested in the bathtub soap dish. Charmin rolled from the dispenser in the bathroom. And on Delmer's dresser I once spotted a bottle of Hai Karate and a tube of Brylcreem!

35

Everything 'Bout the Kitchen Sink

"Please, may I have a cookie?" My second-grade teacher stressed good manners and proper grammar, and I found that Mom appreciated them also.

"Did you wash your hands?" Mom glanced at me as she peeled potatoes at the bigger sink in the kitchen.

"Nah, they aren't even dirty." I held them up. Something gray was encrusted on my fingertips, probably from petting Rex. Plum jam left from breakfast must have attracted barn dust when I searched the hayloft for baby kittens. Mud splotches dappled my arms and colored my fingernails, the results of mixing mud pies.

Hardly worth the waste of time and water, I thought. Besides, I just wanted a cookie; I wouldn't be licking my fingers!

But mother took cleanliness seriously, so I heaved a dramatic sigh and headed to the other sink in the kitchen, the small wash sink attached to the wall near the door. Just tall enough to reach the handles, I leaned in, shut the drain and turned on both faucets. My hands swished in the warm water and my thoughts swirled to my friend's kitchen sink.

Her family didn't have indoor plumbing yet, but they had a different kind of sink. It was a porcelain basin on a table. The best thing about their little sink was the bucket of water up on a shelf. The long handle of a dipper stuck out at the top. When I needed a drink of water, the friend's mom handed me the dipper and I slurped it right down. It was so fun to drink from that dipper! I got thirsty quite often.

I stirred and splashed the warm water and examined the items beckoning from the white shiny surface. To the right in the little indentation was a block of soap. Lifebuoy was printed on the top. I sniffed it and dropped it into the water. My small hands chased it around awhile. Suds topped the little waves. I sang the silly camp song to myself, "I wish I were a little piece of soap…" I fished out the bar and put it back in its place. Another kind sat in a plastic dish on the left. Lava. I rubbed my fingers over it and decided against a sandpaper scrub, though I did try out Dad's nail scrubber brush.

A bit higher sat a thin white block that had a clean smell. I dropped it into the water. It floated. I pushed it down. Up it came! This Ivory was handy; you would never lose the soap.

My eyes lifted to the medicine cabinet, a shallow metal box with a mirror door on the front. I couldn't open it without climbing on the stool, but I had watched Dad, Mom, and the rest of the family and I knew just what was in there.

My hands paddled through the soft bubbles while I imagined all the handy items in that medicine cabinet. Dad's razor, shaving soap and brush huddled in one corner. Polident sat next to them, ready to clean his pop-out teeth. A strong-smelling brown soap bar, Fels Naptha, that Mom used for scrubbing collars and stains, was tucked on the middle shelf.

Prell and White Rain shampoo sat on the bottom, since this sink was the hair-washing station for Mom and the girls.

At the very top were the glass bottles of Mercurochrome, peroxide and Campho Fenique, the first aid medicines for cuts and scrapes. They were smelly and sometimes stung worse than the injury.

The water was cold, so I let it out. The murky liquid left a trail of dirt as it swirled down the drain. I dried my extremely wrinkled hands on the long "roller" towel nearby.

"Thanks, Mom!" I called as I grabbed a cookie and scrambled outside—to play in the dirt!

36

The Light Keeps Shining

I pulled the rocking chair over the carpet and sat directly in front of her. I rested my hands on her knees. Her 104-year-old eyes were not as keen as they used to be. She reached for her hearing aids, and with some difficulty and a bout of device-squealing, she got them adjusted.

"Ah, DeAnn." She leaned forward and placed her cool gnarled hands upon mine. Thus began the highlight of my week.

"I have a joke for you." The jest may have been a one-line pun or a detailed dialog of famous characters on the golf course, but always ended with laughter and often her statement, "I think we need to laugh more."

We talked politics. Though not always on the exact same page, it didn't matter, for we both knew at the end of the book, we hoped for the same things. God and religion and grace entered the conversation. We shared our questions and freely gave opinions. Inevitably, faith and thankfulness came to light.

Family, friends and acquaintances streamed into our visit. Triumphs and tears. We promised to pray and I knew that at our next visit she would report and inquire about those same people.

We shared memories. Her face glowed with love as she spoke of her students in country school and her beloved family. "Oh yes, I remember when..." The expert storyteller held me spellbound.

Always, the dear lady wanted our time to end on a positive note. She believed in celebrating successes. She shared life's miracles, whether in a hospital room or her back yard. Always, I left with a smile, wanting to be a better person.

This column's name is based on Edith Wharton's words. "There are two ways of spreading light: to be the candle or the mirror that reflects it." My dear friend perfectly exemplified the candle—a light shining with laughter, genuine caring, and encouragement. Her positive attitude inspired a hopeful perspective on life. She glowed with unwavering love and loyalty that made a person feel cherished. This woman's example motivated all who knew her to reflect her light in a sometimes-dark-and-scary world—to be the mirrors.

My wish for you is that you have someone like her in your life. Someone dear who brings you light and inspires you to keep shining and reflecting your own heart's brightest light.

Happy 105th birthday in heaven, Ethel!

Ethel the listener, the encourager

37

A Tale of Six Parties

It was the best of times, it was the worst of times, it was the age of awareness, it was the age of questioning, it was the epoch of trust, it was the epoch of doubt, it was the season of patience, it was the season of annoyance, it was the spring of humor, it was the winter of outrage—in short, the time was somewhat like the present. For good or for evil, it was the era of—the party line.

The party line system was common in the rural Midwest, particularly between 1930 and 1970. Copper wires stretched from pole to pole, connecting multiple homes. Up to 20 families shared a single telephone line. These lines were a cost-effective way to connect more phones over large distances. Each subscriber was assigned a distinct ring to their incoming call. These "rings" were a combination of "longs" and "shorts," and rang in to every party on the line. Not only did everyone on the line hear the ring signal, anyone could also overhear conversations simply by lifting their own phone receiver. The phone company frowned on "rubbernecking," eavesdropping on neighbor's chats, but somehow everyone always seemed to know everyone else's business.

When people were talking and someone else on the line lifted their receiver, there was a subtle "click" and at once it became more difficult for the original talkers to hear the conversation. At the same time, everyone involved could hear background sounds from the eavesdropper's home, including breathing.

Growing up in rural South Dakota, we had at least six families on our party line. Overall, the neighbors were pretty considerate, though there were a few exasperating times when we needed to make a call, but the line was busy for what seemed like forever.

In spite of our parents' strict guidelines for our phone use, I am certain that as a teenager I was the source of irritation for others on our line. One such tale may have gone something like this:

"Hello." I grabbed the heavy black handle off its pedestal quickly when our "two longs" chimed. My friend had promised to call after school. The rest of the family was outside, the best of times to be on the phone. Though it had only been an hour since we last talked, critical issues entered the conversation.

"What are you doing this weekend?" After discussing every possible event, I asked about the boys who had to stay after school, the typical punishment in those days. We talked of the teachers involved, the superintendent's threats and our relief that we were not involved in anything so scandalous.

Suddenly, we heard a click. "Ahhh, somebody is listening in," my statement dripped with disgust. "Let's just wait and maybe they will hang up."

Two minutes of breathing left no fewer parties on the line. "Some people are SO inconsiderate," my friend spoke pointedly.

"Yeah," I agreed with a dramatic sigh, though a small voice whispered that my parents would not approve of my phone etiquette either.

At last, a lady's voice interrupted our earth-shattering exchange. "Will you girls please get off the phone? I need to make an important phone call."

More huge sighs accompanied our reluctant goodbyes.

Back then there were no answering machines, so if the caller did not give up, the ringing would continue incessantly. More than once, after counting thirty distinctive ring signals, I lifted our receiver and slammed it back down, ending the noisy summons. Occasionally, the ringing started right up again.

Overall, our experience with party lines was good. We had considerate neighbors. Not everyone was so fortunate. There were horror stories of houses that burned down or people who died because talkers refused to give up the line. Eventually, the parties were phased into private lines. Privacy was a far, far better thing.

But people must have missed all those best of times and worst of times because new and more elaborate forms of social media were invented. And today, everyone still knows everyone else's business!

DeAnn checking for parties on the party line.

38

Maybe You Can Save Them

The blue Ford pickup hurtled into the front yard and skidded to a stop just in front of the gate.

"Dad must have had trouble." A worried frown crossed Mom's face as she waited for her farmer husband to come inside. Timing for field work was critical. A machinery breakdown, sometimes combined with rain, could delay planting, cultivating or harvesting to the point of crop loss. Only the direst of circumstances interrupted Dad and the boys when they were farming.

Cradling his farm cap against his chest, my father walked into the kitchen. With one large hand under the upturned cap, he gently handed it to me. Four green eggs nestled into the warmth of his blue bandanna. "I didn't see the nest." Sadness flashed through his eyes and I realized the mother duck had not survived. "Maybe you can save them." He glanced up at Mom who knew her husband's soft heart. He grabbed a different cap off the hook behind the door and hurried back out to the field.

A small flock of bantams lived in our barn. In spring and early summer, there was often a broody hen that wanted nothing more in life than to hatch eggs and raise babies. Sure enough, a determined little banty was hunkered down in the sheep manger.

Keeping the four eggs as warm as possible, we carried them to a makeshift house, a big wooden box that sat on its side in the shade between the granary and the yard fence. I carefully tucked the eggs into a straw-lined peach crate in the back corner.

At the barn, Mom scooped up the hen that squawked her complaint, but then clucked softly, snuggled into Mom's apron. I slid aside the wooden partition that served as a door to the brooder box. Mother gently set the little chicken down close to the nest. Peeking through the top of the door, we waited. After what seemed like forever, she jumped into the crate, wings outstretched and delicately stepped into the straw. She shimmied down over the eggs, then nudged them under her soft tummy with her beak. At last, she grew quiet. Determined eyes dared anyone or anything to disturb her new nest. I looked up at Mom. She was smiling.

Later that night, we set food and water inside the little house. And we waited. Mom explained that duck eggs needed moisture to keep the shells from getting too hard for the round baby beaks to peck open at hatching time. In the wild, a mother duck might go for a swim, then return to her nest, thus keeping the eggs moist. I knew Mom was preparing me in case the eggs did not hatch, but I still hoped. Every day I peeked in to check on the little black hen.

Finally, 27 days after Dad had brought home the rescued eggs, I thought I heard peeping in the brooder box! I ran to get Mom. We peeked in through the door opening. Three little brown and yellow striped heads poked out from under soft feathers.

The life and times of wild baby ducks on the farm is another story, but they came about because of a hard-working farmer with a big heart. "Maybe you can save them."

39

Rocks of Ages, Part I

The crunch of tires on gravel suddenly changed to the harsh brush of tall grasses underneath. The pickup leaned perilously to the right. Instinctively, I grabbed the side of the seat—anything to hang on to. Dad eased the steering wheel back to the left and guided the '54 Ford back on the road.

A sheepish grin flashed on the driver's face. "Just checking if you were awake."

"Yeah, right!" I laughed and thought of how Mom would have reached for the little handle in the corner window vent and scolded her husband. Told him not to go in the ditch. But like her, my eyes turned to the same window he faced. Tiny leaves had pushed through the earth. Perfect rows of green sparkled in the sunlight.

"Looks like a nice stand of corn." Dad took pride in his fields. Straight rows, healthy crops, few weeds. Suddenly his foot pressed the brake and he stared out in the distance. Over and around a big rolling hill, white and gray objects stuck out of the soil like bad blemishes.

"You and Delmer will have to pick rock." I glared at the horrible things as though they were an enemy about to attack.

"We picked rock last year. Where do they come from?" I recalled Dorothy, Darlene, Delmer and I traipsing through the same field, tossing rocks onto the flat tin, then hauling them to the rock pile at the end of the field.

"Have you studied glaciers in school?" Dad questioned. "Those rocks probably came from Canada 20,000 years ago." I frowned, vaguely remembering that chapter in my social studies book. I had a hard time imagining a gigantic sheet of ice moving over the land, cutting, slicing, then leaving behind rocks it picked up a thousand miles away. Besides, my thoughts in class that day were likely on the book the teacher was reading to the class. *By the Shores of Silver Lake.* Mary, Ma, Carrie and Baby Grace all had scarlet fever. I knew something horrible was going to happen.

Dad was probably wondering why they bothered to send me to school. I set his mind at ease. "Why did that dumb glacier have to dump all it's rocks in our field?"

In spite of my bright, positive attitude, Dad still sent Delmer and me to pick rock. He said it was because those mineral chunks were hard on machinery. But I figured he didn't like the looks of them in his perfectly coiffed fields.

Delmer drove the John Deere 520, pulling the manure spreader behind. I sat in the yellow seat next to him. He eased the tractor onto the grass-covered approach. In the field he shifted down and skillfully maneuvered all wheels between the corn rows. We approached the hill of ill repute. He turned off the tractor and climbed down.

"I'll just sit up here and point out the rocks."

"Funny." My brother knew how to inspire motivation. "Let's go."

We developed a system, each covering a certain number of rows out from the tractor. Stones of every size, shape and color clunked into the manure spreader. Heading to a rather large rock up ahead, my brother called, "DeAnn, drive the tractor up this way."

I froze in my tracks. I had driven the 520. It was fun. Steer, clutch, throttle. Easy peasy! But never had I maneuvered that huge machine through one of Dad's beloved cornfields. "No, Delmer, I can't." Visions of a bare hilltop danced in my head.

"It's time you learned." My brother patiently encouraged me to strive beyond my comfort zone. "Come on. Just do it…sometime today?"

So, I did. Sort of. My hands trembled as I put the tractor in low gear and pushed the clutch lever forward. I watched the bright green plants slide by between the wheels. All went well until…

To be continued.

40

Rocks of Ages, Part II

Continued from last week...

I just needed to drive the tractor up to Delmer and the next group of rocks without running over any corn plants, but I was scared to death. Every turning wheel was a potential killer that needed to be watched: the double tractor wheels in front of me, the big tractor tires beside me, the wheels on the manure spreader behind me. I had to keep them away from the baby corn plants. I could not ruin Dad's beautiful rows.

I swiped the sweat from my eyes with the back of my hand and glanced up at my brother. One hand on his hip and the other balancing a rock on his shoulder like Hercules, he waited. He shook his head and rolled his eyes to encourage me. Not much farther. Maybe I could do this.

But then it happened, my worst nightmare. In what seemed like a split second, giant treads plowed right into the row. I panicked and jerked the steering wheel to the right, only to smash little innocent shoots on the other side!

Eventually, I caught on; the manure spreader followed in the tractor tracks. I stopped next to Delmer and turned off the engine. I scurried off the tractor and ran back to check for damage. Little green spears lay flat against the ground. I felt horrible. I tried to set them up again and pushed soft soil around them.

Delmer said it was OK, that I hadn't hurt many plants. "They might come back and grow just fine."

But my conscience niggled at me as it always does. I knew I had to tell Dad. So, that night at the supper table I nervously cleared my throat. "Dad, I ran over some corn plants today when we were picking rock."

My father frowned and turned to Delmer. A chill ran down my spine. I was prepared for a scolding, though as the youngest, most spoiled, I knew it wouldn't be too tough. But I never for a second imagined I might be incriminating my mostly-pretty-good brother.

Delmer swallowed his mashed potatoes. "I figured it was time she learned how to drive in the corn."

I looked Dad straight in the eye, the way he taught us to talk to people. But no words would come. I prayed and tried to will my father not to blame my brother.

Sometimes I think Dad could read my mind. A twinkle flickered in his hazel eyes, but he managed to speak sternly. "Delmer's right. It's time you learned."

Three weeks later, I again rode shotgun in the pickup when Dad was checking the crops. As we approached the Field of Rocks, I held my breath, hoping my father had forgotten my corn-killing confession.

He glanced over at me, then pulled to the side of the road. Quietly we stared up at the hill together. Perfect rows of green sparkled in the sunlight.

41

Staying Connected

"Stay Connected!" The message called from the clear pocket in front of me through liftoff, turbulence, deceleration, and a rather bouncy landing. The airline obviously wanted me to come back soon for more twisty pretzels.

On these trips to visit California daughter, I sometimes reflect on life in covered wagon days. When a mother hugged her daughter goodbye, chances were good they would never see each other again.

It should be easier to stay connected in this day and age, shouldn't it? Airline travel is far more prevalent than when we were growing up. Today, it is the way people travel. Happy to get a window seat, I waited for takeoff. Behind me a baby cried. Young children squabbled. A boisterous high school soccer team filed in. I could tell that most of the travelers were familiar with flying.

Before the flight attendant launched her seat-belt-and-oxygen-mask spiel, nearly everyone had focused on some type of screen before them. I glanced at the person next to me. He was immersed in something on his iPad, ear buds blaring. Friendly chatter was out of the question.

My trips by airplane can be counted on two hands. I still find liftoff amazing and I love watching the ground below. Even the clouds fascinate me. My window shade was one of few that were open.

Growing up on the farm sixty-plus years ago, when the family traveled, we rode in the car. Dad drove. Mom was front passenger. When I was really young, I sat between them and the other kids sat in the back. No air conditioning besides Mom and Dad's front vents and the hand crank windows.

The folks commented on the crops, beautiful yards, trees and livestock. Kids in the back pointed at the changing scenery. "Those trees are huge!" "Look at all the baby colts." Nature fascinated us. There were so many things to see, so much to imagine.

When we drove next to a train, we counted the cars. License plates on passing and oncoming vehicles were better than "Jeopardy."How many South Dakota counties could we spot? Deloris recalls Mom reaching for the map in the glove compartment to show us where the counties were located. (Better than GPS!) It was fun to tally all the different states.

There were no mobile phones then, at least not in our world. No iPads or laptops. No Facebook, Twitter, Instagram or TikTok. Today, billions of people have access to social media platforms. We live in the Age of Technology. We can access information instantly. We can socialize. We can communicate. We can connect.

So, why do some educators say today's students have a difficult time listening and following directions? Why are sharing and cooperating skills waning?

Why are so many people lonely? Government studies report that loneliness is on the rise, especially among younger adults. A book by Jonathan Haidt, *The Anxious Generation,* addresses the present-day crisis in technology. He also tells how we can fix it. I recommend it for every parent, grandparent and adult who cares about the future.

Technology is a wonderful thing. (I would not want to give up flights to visit family or connecting with phone and computer.) Turns out, we just need to learn how to use it. However, we can still keep counting train cars, playing license plate games and just plain talking!

42

A Really Big "Shoo"

It was a Sunday night. February 9, 1964. More than 73 million Americans waited with anticipation. Our family was among those as we sat in the living room in front of our black and white Zenith. Little did we know then how much that awaited performance would affect the world.

Ed Sullivan, host and creator of the variety show, introduced the act simply, "Ladies and gentlemen. The Beatles. Let's bring them on." But the last sentence was completely drowned out by the screaming crowd. On that night, four lads from Liverpool, England, took to the stage and forever changed the course of music history. John, Paul, George and Ringo's songs that night included "I want to Hold Your Hand," "All My Loving," and "She Loves You." Fans went wild. Never before had the world experienced such excitement for a musical performance.

The excitement in our living room did not quite match that of other fans. Mom in her easy chair calmly watched as she crocheted a lace edge on a pillowcase. No verbal comment, but she had a way of wrinkling her nose that made me giggle. I suspected she preferred church music. I am not sure what Dad thought of the music, but he definitely did not approve of the long hair.

Delmer appreciated the group's talent, and he and his friend Neal later added Beatles' songs to their band's repertoire. Dorothy liked the Beatles, but was a loyal Elvis fan. I was really glad she wasn't behaving like the teenage girls on the show. All that shrieking and fainting was a bit much for me as a nine-year-old. The animation level of the studio audience that night was so high that Sullivan feared the other acts would be compromised. He even threatened in jest, "If you don't keep quiet, I'm going to send for a barber!" Dad probably approved of that comment.

Our sister Darlene was in nurses training at a Denver hospital at the time. That same year, she told of a mobbing outside a Denver hotel when the Beatles arrived to perform in concert. Six girls had to be hospitalized after being trampled. One teen bit a police officer who was attempting to control the situation.

The iconic group continued their rocket to stardom on The Ed Sullivan Show. The famous host often opened his show with, "Ladies and gentlemen, we have a really big show," but "show" sounded like "shoo." The broadcast premiered in 1948, originally called "Toast of the Town." Even that first event made history when Rodgers and Hammerstein gave the world a taste of the score of *South Pacific.* Sullivan brought talent of all kinds to the TV screen for 23 years, showcasing entertainers from all over the world. I wonder how many rose to fame after their appearance? How many were inspired to pursue their own careers?

Mr. Sullivan hired a far-reaching band of scouts, but he also had an eye (and ear) for potential fame. His vision proved true for many who became stars after performing on his show.

I wonder if Mr. Sullivan knew how many memories he would create? How many dreams come true? I wonder if he realized how big his "shoo" really was?

43

My, How Time Flies!

"How much longer?" Sitting between Mom and Dad on the more-than-two-hour drive to Lake Traverse, I had asked the question ten minutes ago. I knew better than to ask again, but it seemed like we would NEVER get there. The family trekked to the lake every summer. The trunk was loaded with the essentials: fishing poles, worms, tackle box, cooler full of Mom's fried chicken and potato salad. I couldn't wait to see the fish jumping in the cool blue water! The miles dragged on for what seemed like forever.

Dorothy thought time went slowly every summer. She loved school and social time with her friends. The three months between seemed like much longer to my sister.

Delmer loved those summer days, so the two weeks of Bible School he had to endure right after school got out was endless torture for him. The weekly hour of church every Sunday morning was my definition of suffering. The music was ok, but my six-year-old eyes glazed over during the readings. How could people give their kids names like that? And then speak to them with thee and thou? I tried to focus, I really did. First, I focused on swinging my feet up and down, shiny shoes flashing to the rhythm of the words. Mom put her hand on my knees. Then, during the ten-hour sermon, I caught sight of a fluffy black feather in the lady's hat just in front of me. I wondered if I could sit very still and very softly blow a very gentle breath of very innocent air, and make that feather move. All that wondering turned to trying. Just when that feather flitted, Dad turned to me with a frown. But as he looked back at the preacher, I noticed a tiny twinkle in his eyes. I bet he wondered about that feather too!

When you are a kid, time almost stands still. I remember every November thinking that Christmas would never come. It was the same for birthdays.

During the school year, that last period of the day was the longest. The hands on the big clock moved slower than a sloth. Would the last bell ever ring?

Now that we are a bit older, my siblings and peers all agree: time flies! Destinations are reached in no time. Summers turn to winter and we hardly notice the change in leaf color. Church is over before we know it, even without feathery hats.

And Christmas? Every year, I swear Christmas arrives the day after Thanksgiving.

As much as I hate to admit it, time has not changed. A minute today is the exact same length as a minute 65 years ago. Scientific studies have been done to explain this difference in time perception. Some claim the sensation of differing lapses in time has to do with how our brains process our experiences. As we age, we have feelings of increasing rapidity of time.

A Dr. Ornstein's experiments on humans with experiences in varying complexities led him to conclude that we perceive time as moving slowly when we are given greater amounts of new information. Thus, when we are children, time seems to move in slow-motion because every day, hour and minute our lives give us something new to experience; our brains need more time to process things with which we are not familiar. Thus, time seems to lag.

Well, Dr. Ornstein, if I work very hard and take a lot of fastly-flying time, I can understand your conclusions. But with all due respect, I still uphold my own theory. I still believe that the older we get, the more experiences we have shared. Through the good times and bad, we have learned how very precious life is, every single minute.

Darlene, Donald, Deloris, Dorothy, Delmer (front). Ready for a road trip!

44

Come on in—Sit a Spell

"Come on in! Mabel will put the coffee on." Dad extended the invitation. It didn't matter who the visitors were or what they did, hospitality was extended. And, almost always, they accepted.

The kitchen table served as the gathering place. "Pull up a chair." Dad nodded and removed his seed corn cap. Mom smiled graciously and filled the coffeepot. Depending on the time of day, some type of food appeared on the table. Mid-morning or afternoon, cookies from the cookie jar in the corner were placed neatly on a pretty glass serving plate. If Mom didn't have fresh homemade cookies, she was a bit embarrassed. She may even have apologized, but at least there were store bought. No-food was not an option.

From the hutch in the corner, Mom got out one of the cream and sugar sets. In Scandinavian Hosting 101, her mother had taught her that you always have cream and sugar available for guests.

The Fuller Brush guy, the Avon lady, or the vacuum cleaner salesman sat right down and chatted a bit before they got out the latest catalog or promotional brochure. The neighbor who wanted to set up corn shelling, the uncle who was driving by and thought he would stop in were greeted with a handshake and "Let's have a cup of coffee."

Occasionally, someone pulled into our driveway at 11:45 AM. Dad greeted them as he and the boys returned from the field. "Come in for dinner. Mabel scrounged up something, though the neighbors haven't brought in much lately. Everyone knew he was joking, but I wondered what Mom thought. She worked hard to have good meals on the table, no matter who was there to eat them. Those were the meat-and-potatoes days.

Dad and Mom both noticed and commented after the fact that one salesman began making a habit of showing up just before noon. He knew where to get a good meal! One such time, Mom had pork chops, frying one for each person in the family. She whispered to me as I set another plate on the table, "You and I will share a pork chop." Liking Mom's pork chops a lot, I wasn't too thrilled with the arrangement. (I would have failed the Hosting class.) She made a coating with corn flake crumbs and fried them to golden perfection. I watched the guy happily plunk the biggest one onto his plate. I even hoped for some stray breading left on the plate. No luck with that either! But I knew better than to complain out loud. When we had guests, we treated them right.

During that same era, a TV show aired that demonstrated similar hospitality. Our parents had the genial genes long before The Beverly Hillbillies, but they enjoyed watching the show. Granny also made sure there was plenty of food for her family. Jed, Jethro, and Ellie Mae savored Granny's special dishes. "Mmmm, Granny. Them's might fine vittles!"

Granny rustled up her hearty and unusual specialties: fried possum and "heavenly hash." This was a mixture of grits, catfish, hog jowls and gopher gravy. Mr. Drysdale and his secretary, Miss Jane Hathaway, attempting politeness while trying to hide their revulsion, always declined Jed and Granny's invitation to join them for dinner.

"The Beverly Hillbillies" series was a big hit on American television. It ran from 1962 to 1971. It ranked among the top 20 most-watched shows for eight of its nine seasons, twice reaching the number one spot with their "heaping helping of hospitality."

Unlike the Clampetts, guests seldom refused our folks' invitations. Could be people back then preferred cornflake coating to gopher gravy.

One of Mom's cream and sugar sets, a wedding gift. Thank you, Susan Nash for the photo.

45

Give Them Something to Talk About

"Come sit by me. We need to visit." Grandma patted the chair next to her at our kitchen table. "What have you been doing this summer?" Sincere interest shone in her faded blue eyes. Soon the conversation changed courses. "That reminds me of when I was young." And Grandma told stories.

Even as a youngster I knew times had changed; our parents and grandparents led far different lives than we. I loved hearing about the old days, from the war and one-room schools to a mean goose that guarded the homestead. The memories she shared remain with me, a part of history, but more importantly, she made me feel special. She took the time to sit and talk to me, one on one, eye to eye.

When we visited family, we youngsters were usually included in the conversation or activities. Dorothy recalls Grandpa Anderson lighting his pipe and then holding the match for her to blow out. "Come and see my flowers." Grandma smiled as she headed for the door.

My sister also remembers visiting our uncles, who were some of the first to purchase a television set when the invention first came out. They proudly led Dorothy and Darlene to the living room, turned on the switch and fiddled with the station knob. Sometimes there was just "snow," but when there was any kind of picture and sound, everyone was impressed.

Aunt Julia never had her own children, but always treated her nieces and nephews royally, at least that's how we felt. Deloris reminisces fondly of "playing" Julia's player piano. Our feet stretched for the foot pedals, turning the perforated music roll in front of us while the keys magically played by themselves. On Julia's birthday, she made the treats: homemade buns for sandwiches. The adults drank coffee, but this aunt made the kids "nectar." Made from a concentrate she purchased from the Watkins man, it was even better than Kool Aid!

Julia kept Spearmint gum in her purse and generously offered us a stick whenever we sat next to her. One spring when we visited, she pulled on her heavy coat and boots. "You've got to come to the barn and see the new babies. One ewe had triplets!"

When Mom and her sisters got together, the conversation was lively. My siblings and I affectionately remember their giggles, especially Aunt Ida's. On occasion, they got to laughing so hard tears streamed down their faces. It's funny how I cannot recall what they were talking about, but I can see and hear their merriment like it was yesterday.

In this day and age, it is easy to be distracted by technology. Last week a peer commented, "I stopped to see the grandkids and they sat and stared at their phones the whole time. Didn't say a word."

But there are still plenty of good times going on, lots of memories being made. Going to the fair, checking the back yard for bird nests, fishing, ballgames, pontoon rides, picnics, looking at photo albums, baking cookies and many more.

We may have to work on it, but we can all help make memories. Our loved ones will recall these days in 50 years. "I remember going to Grandma and Grandpa's. It was so cool."

Let's give them something to talk about!

Grandson Jackson uncapping honey. Making memories at Grandma's house.

46

Darker Than Night

Darkness surrounded me. No moon or stars lit the path that led through our farm yard to the brooder house. "Check for chickens roosting in the trees, then shut them in for the night," Mom instructed, though I knew the drill. But usually, a bit of daylight remained or Delmer walked with me. Tonight, I was on my own.

My imagination ran wild anyway, but being all alone on a pitch-dark night made it shift to overdrive. What were the worst critters I may have encountered? Maybe a wayward racoon or skunk. But my eight-year-old brain conjured up horrible creatures lurking in the blackness. If Simon and Garfunkel would have conferred with me that night, they would have written "Hello darkness, my old enemy…" John Wheeler would have coined the term, "black hole" a couple years sooner. There is nothing darker than night to a child.

I aimed the flashlight beam at the ground in front of me and to all sides, catching every shadow, every movement in the grass or branches. My heart pounded in rhythm with my feet padding on the ground. The wheel on the windmill creaked eerily. Eyes watched me from the water tank. The cow slurped loudly, then lowed a sad moan and turned back to the pasture. Something skittered across the path to the granary. The walk was only fifty yards, but it seemed like a mile.

Finally, I reached the small white building. Hopefully, all of the young pullets had made their curfew and were safe inside on the roosts. No such luck. Two teens had decided to have a slumber party in the tree under the stars. Their white feathers reflected in the light. I gave the branch the biggest shake I could muster and both crash-landed. It took them a few seconds, but they recovered and scurried into the small door. I slammed it shut and hooked the latch. Mission accomplished, I raced back to the house.

My siblings recall their memories of nighttime excursions. One night Mom needed cobs for the cook stove. Delmer trudged through the snow to the old shop where a supply of dry corncobs awaited in case the outside pile was inaccessible. In the darkness he set the flashlight to shine before him. Something moved in the corner, making a scritching sound. Two pairs of beady eyes glared at him. Rats! Never had a bushel basket been filled so fast!

Before Delmer's time, it was Dorothy's job to keep the cob box filled. One day she forgot. It was after dark when Mom chided my sister. The stove needed fuel and it was Dorothy's responsibility to bring it in, even in the dark. The stack of cobs left from corn shelling seemed much farther away that night. Dorothy imagined skunks and monsters of all kinds lurking on the path, ready to pounce. Blond braids flying, she raced through the night to the corn crib, filled the basket and hurried back inside. My sister never again forgot to bring in the cobs.

Funny how darkness was darker three or four decades ago than it is today. It was 10:00 last night when I realized I had forgotten my little basket of eggs outside. They were on the picnic table just in front of the chicken house. I knew that if I left them out, they would be gone by morning, so I headed out in the dark for my four little brown eggs. It's only twenty yards to my chicken coops. I grabbed the flashlight and aimed the beam all around, just in case. I snatched the eggs and hurried back inside. It was not nearly as dark as when I was a kid, but my imagination still runs wild!

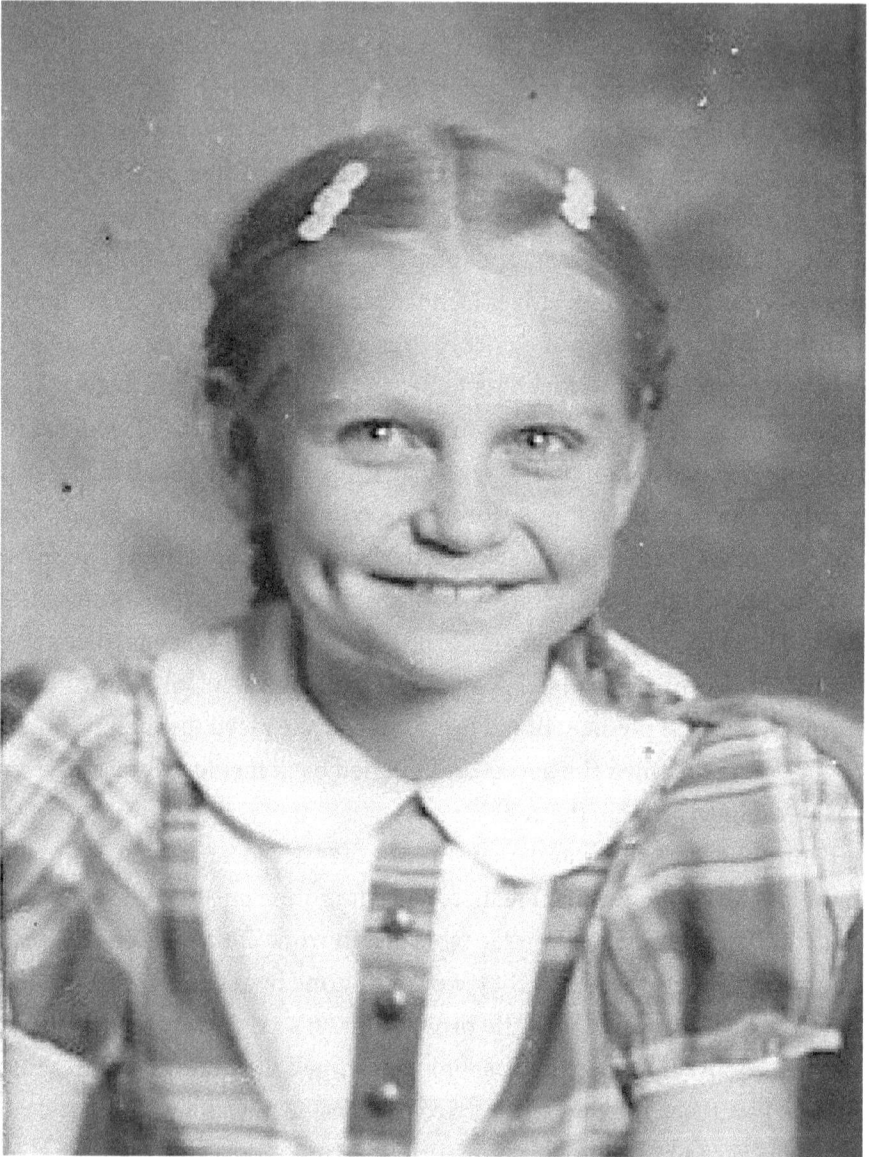

Dorothy

47

The Door to Happiness is Always Ajar

Or maybe a jar? A jar of dill pickles? How about bread and butter or sweet lime? Yellow bean, crab apple, cinnamon apple rings, watermelon rind, or beet? All of these kinds of pickles and probably more lined our farm pantry shelves. When we were blessed with produce, Mom stashed it away and pickles provided another food for her family.

Current nutritional studies concur that pickles and such fermented fare are good for us. The colorful concoctions on Mom's relish tray had benefits we didn't even know about, mostly related to improved gut health. Those sour, sweet, spicy chunks of veggies and fruit are laden with probiotics, which are good bacteria that affect the gut microbiome. Yes, the reality is jarring that pickles can improve digestion, increase nutrient absorption and build a stronger immune system. Crunching on a pickle can boost mental health and reduce inflammation! Life can be hard, dill with it!

Our mother likely had never heard of gut biomes or probiotics, but she took pickle making seriously. Her children and later, grandchildren, relished those homemade delicacies. And just as important, when we were blessed with abundance, it was crucial to make use of it. Our parents grew up during the Great Depression and the thirties. Living through times when food was rationed and crops withered and died in drought, taught them to store up during the good years. It also taught them that nothing should be wasted.

I remember Mom wielding her butcher knife into a giant watermelon. A

131

crack split before the knife and pink droplets oozed out along with a sweet aroma. Mom smiled. "That means it's a good melon." She set the two halves on the cutting board. She smiled again. "There's a thick rind. Perfect for pickles!"

Deloris carries on our mother's pickle-making tradition with unbeatable beet pickles, made with love and shared with loved ones. Dorothy slices cucumbers and onions every year for a batch or two of Mom's refrigerator pickles, which she also shares.

Last night I poured brine over three quarts of cute little cucumbers that will soon become dill pickles for kids and grandkids. Five large, nearly-yellow cukes waited in the bucket. I was about to set them by the door; the chickens rate them right up there with meal worms. But then I thought of how Mom taught us to make use of our blessings. And I thought of how the grandkids would smile when I opened the jar.

I sliced those cucumbers, packed them into an old green two-quart jar and poured brine over them. After all, nothing should be wasted. And the door to happiness may not be a jar, but those jars of memories teach us to relish every moment!

Mom's Refrigerator Pickles

Bring to a boil:

2 cups white vinegar

2 cups sugar

¼ cup canning salt

¾ tsp. turmeric, optional

¾ tsp. celery seed

¾ tsp. mustard seed

Slice cucumbers and onions to fill two quart jars. Pour brine over cukes. Let cool. Refrigerate. Enjoy. Share.

48

The Stories Woven into Our Lives

It sent us out into the world to whatever adventure awaited us. It welcomed us into a safe place of warmth and love.

It was not the first of its kind, nor would it be the last. As the youngest in the family, it is what I remember during most of my growing up years. Mom had made it long before my time and it served its purpose faithfully. Its job was likely overlooked by all of us except Mother; it was literally stomped upon and expected to soak up snow and catch dirt. Lowly, but extraordinary, it saved work.

The edges were frayed and one strip had worked loose in the wash. "It still does its job," Mom said as I helped her lift the dripping mass over the fence to dry. It was far too bulky to go through the wringer.

Years before, Mom had gathered up what was left of old jeans and overalls, the parts between the patches and holes. Even these should not be wasted. She had cut them in strips, sewn them together and rolled them into balls for their final purpose, maybe the most important of all, the rug in front of the door.

Dad had constructed a simple frame of wood and nails. On cold evenings when the South Dakota sun gave us more time inside, Mom would haul out the frame and the strips of cloth that were destined to their final job. Sometimes she bought strong string that she fastened back and forth over the nails. She called it warp. But the rug I remember had no colored string.

She wove the strips over and under each other.

Later, I stood beside her as she made more rugs. These were cotton prints, made from worn out pajamas and shirts and dresses. She showed me how to weave the strips together. "This one will be pretty," she smiled as the colors created their own pattern. Probably after I had flown the coop, Mom set out to make a unique throw rug made totally of old slips and other unmentionables. These should not be wasted either! The rug is mostly white with subtle hues of pink and tan. It greets my bare feet every morning as I slide out of bed.

Each rug was made with love out of the fabrics that had clothed her family over the years, but the heavy, step-worn mat next to the door worked the hardest. It grabbed dirt and other typical farm materials from our shoes so they did not track into the house.

The rug was the stopping spot. Leaning into the kitchen, snow melting from Dad's boots, he would call to our mother. "Can you fill this bottle with milk replacer? That cow still won't take her calf."

I remember standing on that piece of woven comfort with blood oozing from the scrape on my knee. "Mom, can you please get me a bandaid?" which of course turned into a cleaning-out-the-sand session after my bike bucked me off.

If rugs or other objects could talk, they could tell of the threads that wove us into what we are today. A young couple stepping toward their future with little more than a rug and a few sticks of furniture. Little feet walking into the world to new adventures, happy and scary. A teen treading softly so as not to wake the folks—ten minutes after curfew. The first date, but the right one. Tiny feet parallel to big ones, hands joined above to take on the world.

Search deep into your heart's memories. Find something precious bound inside, unlace the strands of your tapestry and tell the stories. As wise Pericles, the guy with the helmet, advised 400 years BC, "What you leave behind is not what is engraved in stone monuments, but what is woven into the lives of others."

49

A Drive Down Memory Lane

Care centers across the country carry on a weekly ritual; they take residents out on a drive through the country. Pull up the van, engage the lift. Wheelchairs, walkers and canes are standard equipment. The seniors settle in for two hours of cornfields, farmhouses, bent windmills, cattle grazing, children playing and hundreds of other sights. Always, they smile.

Growing up on our South Dakota farm, we never turned down an invitation to ride along for a drive. Sunday dinner settled, dishes done, Dad would look at Mom and reach for his cap. "Want to go for a drive?" Mom took off her apron and headed for the car with one or all of the family following.

Dad checked the crops. At the cornfield just up the road, he pulled over and walked into the rows. Minutes later, he was back in the driver's seat and Mom cradled three ears of not-quite-dented corn in her lap. He might check the oat field to see how it was heading out. Farther from home, the folks viewed the neighbors' fields and pastures. "Nice looking cattle." The baby calves looked the nicest to me.

Inevitably, the scenes evoked memories. Dad recalled the Hereford bull that always jumped the fence. Every year, at least two calves came far sooner than planned. When the oats turned golden, Mom told of how they harvested grain when she was young, the cutting, binding and threshing. Threshing crews traveled the country for the harvest. Mom and her sisters and our grandma fed the crew, and how they did eat! In the backseat, we imagined those old-time activities and stored them up for the future.

New farm homes led to stories about that family. The man lost his hand in the corn picker, but it didn't stop him. He farmed for years and bought up more land. His son and family lived at the home place now.

A deserted house with the porch roof caving in elicited Mother's memory. "I worked there one summer and helped take care of the kids. Made 75 cents a week."

Farther on, Dad slowed near an open place in a field. "That's where I grew up." The buildings were gone, but his memories remained. "The neighbor boys would come on Sundays and we played baseball over there. We even played some town teams. We were pretty good."

The sights were common, but the stories kept us at the edge of our seat. Not all the drives were on Sundays. After a windstorm, Dad would drive around all the pastures. If a branch fell on the fence, he would find a place to count the herd. Likely, at least one cow and calf had decided to check if the grass was greener on the other side. This resulted in a mini-roundup of patient cowpokes hollering and wildly waving our arms at the bold bovines, calling them intelligence-insulting names.

A drive down "Memory Lane" can help us recall past experiences and moments, both blissful and bittersweet. Remembering those stored-up memories requires the triggering of a retrieval cue, like a drive through the country. Flashbacks fill our brains.

So, load up the family and take a drive. Remember the moments. Tell the stories. Chances are, they will be told again in the future on another trip down Memory Lane. Chances are, someone will smile.

50

Try it! You'll Like it!

"Just eat one bite. You need to try it." It was one of the rules at our supper table when we grew up on the farm. Most often, the rule applied to vegetables. Asparagus, cooked spinach, carrots. We were expected to put one spoonful on our plate. Of course, we had to eat that spoonful, for another rule was "no dessert unless you clean up your plate." Never did we have to be told we had to "try" dessert!

Our family raised as much of our food as possible. With six children, Mom made sure the basement was stocked with gunny sacks of potatoes and many jars of canned beans, carrots and corn. Pickles, jams, jellies and juices also lined the shelves. We helped grow and preserve it. We ate it and liked it, mostly.

In my latest "what do you remember?" text to siblings, I asked what foods they did not like as children, but possibly enjoy eating now as adults. Dorothy doesn't remember any foods she didn't like. Though our mother was a great cook, the rest of us had some nose-wrinklers.

Deloris, Delmer and I did not like asparagus. In the spring, we loved hunting the shelter belt with Mom for asparagus patches, but eating it was not quite so pleasant.

To state it mildly, the three of us did not relish liver and onions. I rated them number one on the yuck-ometer.

Delmer detested scalloped cabbage. Dad strongly encouraged Delmer to eat some. Delmer liked it less. I loved it! Maybe it's the Swede in me; if you add enough butter and cream, anything tastes good!

Obviously, we never tried that with sauerkraut. Ours fermented in a wood-covered crock in the basement. Sometimes Mom would send me down to scoop out a kettle-full for supper. As the youngest, most spoiled child in the family, I am pretty sure I stated my distaste for the task as well as the smelly, fermented shreds.

Today, much older and hopefully a pinch wiser, I love sauerkraut. In years of plentiful garden cabbages, I've been known to pack away a few jars myself. I have also changed my tastes in the cuisine category for liver and onions; it's become one of my favorite January meals. These days, my siblings and I all love asparagus.

Why do our food fancies fluctuate as we grow older? Is there a reason why grossest grub morphs to favorite feasts?

Researchers claim that young children possess more sensitive taste sensations than adults. Thus, the bitterness of veggies may seem overpowering to a child. Have you ever seen the look on a baby's face with the first spoonful of solid food? Makes me think researchers have a point. However, to assume that as we grow old, we can't taste anything anyway, so we just think everything is yummy—well that's just insensitive!

Nutritional psychologists theorize that repeated exposure to a food, even if initially disliked, can lead to liking. The more familiar our taste buds become with something, the more palatable it becomes.

We can whip up our own theories of why we like foods now we hated as children. I prefer to think that there is some hidden thread, some unconscious need to connect to our childhood that causes us to reconsider. We remember that our parents wanted us to like foods they knew were good for us. Our hearts open our minds.

Maybe the old Alka-Seltzer commercial had a point: "Try it. You'll like it!" It's food for thought.

51

That's the Way the Cookie Crumbles

I am a cookie snob. No need to stroll through the cookie aisle of the grocery store. Sometimes I consider all the additives that allow those plastic packages to sit for months or more, but mostly I don't like the taste. Even the fresh, bakery-made confections have little appeal. This narrow- minded attitude likely goes back to our mother.

There was nothing like jumping off the school bus on a cold winter's afternoon and being greeted at the door with the heavenly scent of fresh-from-the-oven chocolate chip cookies. Or peanut butter, oatmeal raisin or molasses cookies. Some of Mom's recipes were passed down from her mother, but she searched magazines and newspaper columns. Occasionally, her head bent next to the radio and pencil in hand, she added ideas to her repertoire. Mom was one smart cookie!

She often made Dad's favorites. I can see her grin as she watched her husband thoroughly enjoy every chewy morsel. He loved raisins and other fruits. Mom or one of the girls often carried prune drop cookies in a bucket to the farmers working in the fields. It was part of their afternoon "lunch."

Mom and her daughters kept the cookie jar stocked most of the time, and all of us were frequently caught with our hand in the cookie jar. Once in a while a package of cookies made it into the cart at the store. Likely, Dad was the culprit. Crisp ginger snaps, frosted oatmeal and Fig Newtons were some of his choices. Mom would allow me to dip the crunchy ones in her coffee, which was a perfect pairing. Dad would munch down a few of the fig bars and offer me one. Oh, no, those seedy things wrapped in cardboard were not for me!

Cookies convey a compelling history, Fig Newtons in particular. British immigrants introduced the fig roll to America. Possibly inspired by these concoctions, a Philadelphia baker, Charles Roser, developed his own recipe which he sold to a company in Newton, Massachusetts. Thus, the Newton part. Today the cookies are still popular, but the "fig" part has been dropped from the name. Why? Because there are now other flavors: strawberry, raspberry, blueberry and mixed-berry. My tough cookie brain will not allow this mix up. "Darn tootin' I like mixed-berry Newtons?" That's just distasteful!

The love of cookies helped Americans endure the hardships of the Great Depression. Children were known to gather in a circle on the floor and chant, "Who stole the cookie from the cookie jar?" The youngsters took turns accusing each other of stealing from an imaginary cookie jar. A playful call-and-respond ensues. The rhythm and rhyme of the jolly jingle provided respite in hungry times and also a fun game in later years.

Today, Cookie Monster still approves of the treats of every kind. "C is for cookie, that's good enough for me."

"Me too" is my cookie cutter response because lately I have been having a hankering for fig Newtons. Actually, a package mysteriously appeared in my grocery cart last week; I must have been thinking of Dad. What is left of the resealable pack waits in my freezer. Somehow, they no longer taste like seedy things wrapped in cardboard.

"Life is too short for bad cookies," according to Blond Amsterdam. Secret recipe: if you have never heard of Blond Amsterdam, don't let your tummy hurt, we are all still very smart cookies!

Dad's Favorite Prune Drop Cookies

1 cup white sugar

1 cup brown sugar

2/3 cup butter

2 eggs

1 tsp vanilla

½ cup milk, sweet or sour

1 tsp soda

1 tsp baking powder

1 cup cut prunes

3 ½ cups flour

1 tsp salt

1 tsp cinnamon

½ cup chopped nutmeats, optional

Cream sugar and butter. Add beaten eggs and vanilla. Add milk in which soda has been dissolved. Add prunes. Add flour that has been sifted with remaining dry ingredients. Mix just until moistened. Add nuts if desired. Drop by spoonfuls on cookie sheet. Bake 12 to 15 minutes or until lightly browned in moderate oven.

Prune Drop Cookies

2 cups brown or white sugar or half brown and half white. 2/3 cup butter or butter Crises. 2 eggs, 1 teaspoon Vanilla, 1/2 cups milk, sweet or sour, 1 teaspoon soda, 1 cups cut cooked prunes. 3 1/2 cups flour, 1 teaspoon baking powder, 1 teaspoon Cinnamon, 1/4 teaspoon salt, 1/2 cup chopped nut meat, cream sugar and shortening; add beaten eggs and Vanilla, mix thoroughly. Add milk in which soda has been dissolved. add prunes, add flour sifted with baking Powder cinnamon and salt, Stir in nut meat. Drop by spoonfuls on pan. Bake 12 to 15 minutes in moderate oven. Makes about 50 cookies   one of Julia Anderson's receipts.

Salted Peanut cookies

1 cup white sugar, 1 cups brown sugar, 2 eggs, 1 cup butter or butter Crises. 1 3/4 cup flour, 1 teaspoon soda, 1 teaspoon baking powder 1 teaspoon Vanilla, 1 cup salted peanuts. Mix in order given. Form into balls, place on cookie sheet and press with a fork. Bake at 350° for 10 to 15 min.

Starlight Mint Surprise cookies

Sift together 3 cups flour, 1 teaspoon soda 1/2 teaspoon salt. Cream. 1 cups butter (half shortening maybe used) add gradually 1 cups sugar 1/2 cup brown sugar. Cream well. Blend in 2 eggs unbeaten 2 Tablespoon Water, 1 Teaspoon Vanilla, beat well, add dry ingredients; mix thoroughly. Cover and refrigerate at least 2 hours. 1 package solid chocolate mint wafers. Enclose each wafer in about 1 tablespoon of chilled dough on baking sheet about 2 inches apart. Bake at 350° oven for 10 to 12 minutes. Makes about 4 1/2 dozen cookies.

From the recipe book Mom wrote out to give to family

52

A Moment in Time

It happened more than 60 years ago, yet I can see it as clearly as if it were yesterday. My fingertips feel the warmth. My eyes see her smile. I can hear the tenderness in her voice.

I ran my fingers over the dark veins that protruded from the top of her hand. My tanned pudgy hand lightly covered hers as I took in the crooked fingers with small knobs on the first joints of both index fingers. I wondered why my mother's hands were so different than mine. She must have read the questions in my eyes. She smiled a wise smile, likely having heard the same from her other five children. "I'm getting old," she stated, her light blue eyes shining with amusement. Though she was only in her late forties, she understood a child's perspective.

"Do they hurt?" I asked, for I loved Mom dearly. Her smile remained as she shook her head, then took up the embroidery hoop and needle to continue my lesson.

One moment in time. I sometimes question why this long-ago-scene, this image of my mother's hands remains so vivid in my mind.

My sisters remember when I first came home from the hospital as a baby. Mom bathed me on the table in the warm kitchen, gently rubbing a washcloth over my face and under my chin. They saw and felt a mother's love, especially in her hands.

Her hands kept us safe. Dorothy reminisces of Mom's hand reaching for

Dorothy's small hand to cross the wide street in De Smet. Mom squeezed harder as they crossed. The little girl felt safe.

Sometimes I spotted small welts and bruises on our mother's hands. I knew from watching what had caused them. Fat Plymouth Rock hens provided our family with eggs. Every summer, several went broody. They sat on the nests, glaring with beady eyes, clucking and defying anyone to take the eggs hiding under their feathers. Mom never would have considered using a stick or grabbing the critter behind the neck and throwing her out. She simply reached her hand under that grumpy old hen and carefully removed the eggs. In the process, the old biddy inflicted wounds with her sharp beak.

Seemingly oblivious to heat, Mom might remove a hot waffle or flip a strip of bacon in the frypan. She must have doubted the necessity of the lefse stick. Fingers worked just as well.

Mother's hands sewed her family's clothing, darned socks, kneaded bread dough, plunged into hot bleach water, and dug in garden dirt. They could wield a rolling pin, butcher knife, potato fork and scoop shovel, all in the same day.

They created beautiful things, embroidering pillowcases and towels, crocheting tablecloths and lace edges. They sewed aprons and quilts, most to be shared with loved ones.

Those loving, patient, tough, strong, creative hands wrote letters to children at camp or college, knowing when love and encouragement were needed.

As I write this, I look at my own hands. Dark veins protrude. Crooked fingers have small knobs on the joints. That moment in time, my vision of our mother's hands endures in my mind as clear and powerful as ever. I think today I know why. Thank you, Mom.

II

About the Author

DeAnn (Wolkow) Kruempel grew up on a farm near De Smet, South Dakota, the sixth child of Harrison and Mabel Wolkow. She attended school at Erwin and De Smet. She married Vicar Robert Kruempel and lived in Benedict, North Dakota, and Toeterville, Akron, and Missouri Valley, Iowa.
The author worked in school and public libraries for more than 30 years before retiring in 2022. She lives near Logan, Iowa, enjoying time with children and grandchildren.

III

Thank you, siblings!

Thank you to my siblings, Deloris, Darlene, Dorothy and Delmer for sharing memories and supporting me in writing endeavors. I often think of our brother, Donald, who would have remembered more than any of us.
Whether humor, adventure, love or hope, your input adds immensely to the stories!

IV

Also by DeAnn (Wolkow) Kruempel

Promises to Keep
Promises Challenged
Promises Strengthened
Promises in Courage
Promises Under Fire
(Historical Fiction Series)

Once Upon a Midwest Sunset
Putting on the Big Boots
Back to Forward
Leaving a Trail
(Collections of the stories published each year in the respective columns.)
All books are available on Amazon.
Contact the author at deannkruempelauthor@gmail.com

www.ingramcontent.com/pod-product-compliance
Lightning Source LLC
Chambersburg PA
CBHW052342100426

42736CB00047B/3407